Unlocking the Scriptures for You

REVELATION
Alger M. Fitch, Jr.

From The Library of Greg Cheatham

**STANDARD
BIBLE STUDIES**

STANDARD PUBLISHING
Cincinnati, Ohio   40113

Unless otherwise noted, all Scripture quotations are taken from *The Holy Bible, New International Version,* © 1973, 1978, 1984 by the International Bible Society. Used by permission of Zondervan Bible Publishers and the International Bible Society.

Sharing the thoughts of his own heart, the author may express views not entirely consistent with those of the publisher.

Library of Congress Cataloging in Publication data:

Fitch, Alger Morton.
    Revelation.

    (Standard Bible Studies)
    1. Bible. N.T. Revelation—Commentaries.
I. Title. II. Series.
BS2825.3.F58   1986   228'.07   85-27732
ISBN 0-87403-173-7 (pbk.)

TABLE OF CONTENTS

PREFACE... 7
INTRODUCTION
   Questions That Give Perspective..................... 11
CHAPTER ONE
   The Perspective of Preaching
   "The Word of God and the Testimony of Jesus" 25
CHAPTER TWO
   The Perspective of Opposition
   "Your ... Companion in the Suffering" 39
CHAPTER THREE
   The Perspective of Advance
   "Your ... Companion in the ... Kingdom"............ 59
CHAPTER FOUR
   The Perspective of Endurance
   "Your ... Companion in the ... Patient Endurance" ... 77
CHAPTER FIVE
   The Perspective of Universal Worship
   "On the Lord's Day ... in the Spirit ... a Voice" 95
CONCLUSION 111

PREFACE

The Book of Revelation can be read aloud in an hour and a half. It contains twenty-two chapters, four hundred fourteen verses, nine thousand eight hundred thirty words, but only one main point: Christ will lead his church to victory!

Revelation was not written to cause fright in the reader, but rather to instill confidence. The same Jesus who sent the church on the mission of making "disciples of all nations" (Matthew 28:19), is revealed to be with the congregations as they carry out their Heavenly assignment in a resistant world. This last book in the New Testament makes clear that, in fulfilling its mission, the church will face harsh conflict and dreadful suffering, but will achieve certain victory.

It would be a mistake to be hasty and rush close to the book of Revelation, with magnifying glass in hand, ready to study particular brushstrokes in some corner of the painting. (Who are the 144,000? What does 666 mean?) We ought first to stand back and to see from a distance the divinely inspired mural in its wholeness. What impress is made on the mind by the bright hues of hope and stormy black-cloud contrasts of history? We see radiant angels in white descend from Heaven and ugly frogs arise from the smoke of the abyss. We hear trumpets sound and angelic choirs sing. One moment, the scene is as raging as wild waves in a tempest. Next, the eye rests on a different sight, where all is at peace and the sea is calm as glass. Unsure as you may be about the meaning of any particular chapter and verse, you have certainty that Christ is the Lord of history. Whatever roadblock the dragon casts into the way of the church, Jesus' presence assures the success of the mission. Should single battles be lost in the struggle for the minds of men, the war will be won by the armies of the King of kings.

Be reminded that the earliest believers in Ephesus, Laodicea, or Sardis did not read private copies of a printed book of Revelation. They did not have mimeographed lessons for a six-months' study intended to result in a clear, detailed chronology of future world history. Instead, they heard John's letter read to a gathered assembly of believers on a Lord's Day. And they went home with one point crystal clear in their minds. What the first Bible prophecy of Genesis 3:15 said in brevity, the last book of prophecy described in more detail: For the people of God, there will be conflict, suffering, and victory.

Often the opening chapter of a Bible book contains a key-verse that unlocks the following pages. Revelation does not disappoint us in this regard. Revelation 1:9, 10 contains five key ideas to be developed by John in the succeeding chapters. He talks of "suffering," "kingdom," "patient endurance" or loyalty, the "word of God and the testimony of Jesus," and the "Lord's Day," the Lord's "Spirit," and the Lord's "voice." After an introductory chapter, we will let the Revelation speak for itself on each of these themes.

Questions That Give Perspective

INTRODUCTION

Questions That Give Perspective

The intelligent examination of any book of sacred Scripture ought to begin with a half-dozen preliminary inquiries. These will give the searching mind needed perspective. Rudyard Kipling spoke of the six honest servant men that taught him all he knew. He wrote, "Their names are What and Why and When and How and Where and Who."[1]

To ask these probing questions will help us have a deep respect for this ancient canonical book. To some, it is the wonder book of the Bible. Their first "wonder" is whether it should even have been accepted as Scripture. The next "wonder" is what it means.

The early Tertullian did not believe the writing to be Christian at all, calling it far too Jewish. The recent D. H. Lawrence, in his commentary *Apocalypse* (Penguin Books, 1974), classifies Revelation as the Judas of New Testament writings, betraying the gentle Jesus by making Him to be vindictive. He writes of the Christ in Revelation, "[The] Lamb is a lion in sheep's clothing" (p. 58).

Many others are more akin to John Calvin, who pushed the book aside as beyond his grasp. Calvin set out to write a commentary on every book of the Old and New Testaments. Yet, the famous *Calvin Commentaries* contain no insights on this book that concludes the Christian Bible.

I find myself at the other end of the pendulum swing. Revelation is my favorite book of all the sixty-six volumes of Scripture. While I am quick to admit vast areas of unanswered questions, I find my heart strangely warmed and my hopes set soaring at

---

[1] "The Elephant's Child" (1902), quoted in *Bartlett's Familiar Quotations* (Little, Brown and Co., 1955), p. 819.

11

every reading of this encouraging book. In Revelation, the titles and attributes of Jehovah are shared by Jesus. His death and resurrection are placed at the center of the universe and are determinative of the outcome of world history. The book pulls back the curtain and reveals God's eternal purpose to seek and to save the world deceived by the dragon, Satan. Starting with Christ's crucifixion and resurrection as events of past history, the Revelator, by means of vision, takes us across the years of time. He reveals that the church through struggle will carry out the risen Lord's order to let the whole world know of His grace that they might escape His judgment.

The "Who" Perspective

The book was written by John (Revelation 1:1, 4, 9; 22:8). Using that single name John was sufficient to identify him to the congregations addressed throughout Asia Minor. Early church tradition placed the apostle John in Ephesus, where he ministered until his death. According to this ancient tradition, John the apostle of Christ—one of the intimate inner circle—gave us a Gospel, some epistles, and the book of Revelation. Justin Martyr, Irenaeus, Clement of Alexandria, Origen, Tertullian, Hippolytus, and other church fathers accepted the tradition.

In the Johannine writings, we find common ideas, common terms, and common theology. Jesus is the "Word" (λόγος) in John 1:1; 1 John 1:1; and Revelation 19:13. He is the Lamb in John 1:29, 36 and Revelation 5:6, 8 and 12. In Gospel and apocalypse, there are the antitheses of light and darkness and of truth and falsehood. In both writings, the number seven has high priority (seven signs and seven "I am" statements in the main body of the Gospel; seven beatitudes and seven sections in the Revelation).

The so-called problems raised by critics (over a difference in Greek style or over some literature believed to identify an "elder John" as distinct from the apostle John) are not insurmountable. The apostle Peter refers to himself by the term *elder* in 1 Peter 5:1. Surely the aged John does not lose apostolic authority when he writes to his "little children" (1 John 2:1). When I use different words speaking to a youth group for a bonfire devotion than I used to comfort the bereaved at a funeral the day before, I have not become a different person. John's Gospel appears to have been written in leisure, his Revelation in haste. The first may have been penned by an assistant, the latter by hand in a depressing situation. The one is a devotional Gospel, the other a symbolic *apocalypse* (that is, a special, symbolic form of literature depicting the struggle between good and evil, with a climactic victory for the good).

These critical questions are far from being finally settled. But, in the interim, I choose to go by the jurisprudent assertion that an idea (as well as a man) ought to be considered innocent until proven guilty. That is, the two-thousand-year-old tradition that John the apostle gave us the Revelation should not be abandoned until irrefutable evidence to the contrary pushes that view beyond the realm of reasonable doubt. John the apostle—John the missionary—is the author of the final twenty-two chapters of the New Testament.

The "Where" and "When" Perspectives

The visions that came to John were seen by him while he was on the isle of Patmos (Revelation 1:9). This isle in the Aegean sea was the "Alcatraz" of its time, where Domitian isolated the unwanted from society. This little island is approximately six miles wide and ten or eleven miles long. It is twenty miles off the mainland of Asia Minor and was sixty miles from the city of Ephesus, where John had ministered for possibly forty years. One of the key-verses of Revelation (1:9) clarifies that John was there "because of the word of God and the testimony of Jesus." We will discuss the exact meaning of this later, but notice this: Where is John? Patmos. Why? Because he is a missionary!

Most scholars, but not all, place the date of Revelation in the reign of Domitian. The dates of A.D. 81 to 96 satisfy several requirements. Such a dating fits the tradition recorded by Eusebius. It allows for the decadence in the churches, reflected especially in chapters 2 and 3. It matches Domitian's policy of punishment and exile that left forty-thousand Christians martyred.[2] It corresponds with a special type of persecution from a man who insisted on being addressed as "Lord and God." It was in the last years of his reign that Domitian insisted all his subjects were so to title him, and those who had learned to speak, "Christ is Lord," had then to face death or say, "Caesar is Lord."

---

[2]Revelation 3:10, 13; 17:6; 18:24; 19:2; 20:4

The "Why" Perspective

Luke, in his book of Acts, told of the church's missionary advance into six areas. He finished each section of his report with a statement of how well the mission went in spite of all the difficulties.[3] In much the same way, John, in his book of Revelation, several times traced the progress of the church from the beginning of the mission to the end of time. Under varied imagery, we see Christ's church in the struggle of being true to Christ's command while being opposed at every turn. However, what Luke saw in Acts to be true from A.D. 30 to A.D. 63, John foresaw to be true from the apostolic age to the end of all time. The Lord will be with His church throughout the struggle. In the end, there will be victory. The mission will not be dubbed a failure. The drawn curtain will reveal converts from "every nation, tribe, people and language" (Revelation 7:9). The assurance of this fact is John's reason for writing.

The "What" Perspective
A. *See the Unveiled Christ*

What is revealed in the Revelation? When the curtain is pulled back, what does God want His people to see? Before we behold that which is revealed about tomorrow *by* Christ, the reader in his own day is blessed by what is made known *about* Christ. No Christian will falter when he recalls the almighty and available power from the Lord.

The days of Jesus incarnate were told by John in his Gospel. The eternal Word became flesh and suffered for men to the point of death on the cross. But the end of that account was a glorious resurrection establishing that the crucified Savior was Lord and God. He breathed His Spirit into His witnesses and sent them out to tend His flock. In the book of Revelation, John describes the ascended Lord as He rules over the world.

Before the first seal on the book of the future is broken (Revelation 6:1), the reader has been reminded that the seal of a tomb had been broken earlier by the "Living One" who declared, "I was dead, and behold I am alive for ever and ever!" (Revelation 1:18).

Let no one be misled by some daily press account or a T.V.

---

[3] Acts 6:7; 9:31; 12:24; 16:5; 19:20; 28:30, 31.

newscaster's report that Satan is in control or that God has abandoned His world. Christ has risen and is reigning. After Israel's Egyptian bondage came the exodus. After her exile in Babylon came the return to Palestine. So the crucifixion of Israel's Messiah was not the end of a sad story but the beginning of a glad story. The resurrection led to an ascension and a coronation at the right hand of God. The Revelation opens our eyes to see the conquest of this King who rules from a Heavenly throne. All enemies will fall before Him.

That Jesus is the risen Lord is established in the first chapter of Revelation. Chapters 1 through 3 show Him to be Lord of the church, as chapters 4 through 20 assert Him to be Lord of history. The last two chapters reveal His reign to extend over all the cosmos through all of eternity.

The book title, "The Revelation of Jesus Christ," is doubly fitting, for Christ is both the revealer and the one revealed. The revelation is given *by* Christ. It also makes evident some wonderful facts *about* Him. One such encouraging fact is that the world will not end by the accident of some foolish man in a nuclear age. The end will come when the Lord of history determines. The four horsemen of chapter 6 could not ride (6:1-8) and the destructive winds mentioned in chapter 7 could not blow (7:1) until Christ allowed.

B. See the Unveiled Church

The mirror that revealed Christ in all His glory reflects His church as it is—warts and all. Christians must face it. Their Lord is perfect. His Word is perfect. But while they desire perfection and long for the perfect day, they know better than any outsiders their own shortcomings. Forgiven? Indeed. Perfect? We all quote Paul, "Not that I have already obtained all this, or have already been made perfect, but I press on" (Philippians 3:12). He who needs forgiveness and finds it in Christ can effectively share God's love with others in similar need.

The legitimate desire of Christians in our day to return to the faith and practice of the first-century church must be clearly understood. The early church did not live in a golden age. The flesh and blood followers of Jesus in the times of the apostles were very much like those found in the churches today. What they did have were letters from Christ's ambassadors to establish for all time the norm for Christian life and teaching. The

Corinthian church was in some bad ruts, but Paul's letter called them to the true path. The seven congregations named in Revelation 1 through 3 had points of both commendation and condemnation. Yet, they were Christ's lampstands, and their leaders were stars in His hand. They would receive letters from Him because they belonged to Him and because He wanted them to keep the gospel flame burning.

Think of these seven churches as arms on a giant candelabrum covering the Roman province of Asia. Each city is between twenty-five and fifty miles from the one previously named. Each church has the oil of the Spirit resulting in the flaming gospel light. John likely had toured these churches again and again from his base in Ephesus.

As you mentally visualize the churches as a giant candelabrum, the outer arms or branches are the first and last churches in the list, that is, Ephesus and Laodicea. They are in great danger. There is little or no good in Laodicea, and Ephesus has "forsaken [its] first love," a condition that might well cancel the good they had done. As you move inward from both ends of your imagined candelabrum, arms two and six (Smyrna and Philadelphia) represent excellent congregations with nothing wrong in them. They are persecuted and missionary minded, leaving little time to get into spiritual trouble. This leaves three churches in the center. They are half-and-half or so-so congregations with a mixture of weaknesses and strengths (Pergamum, Thyatira, Sardis).

If there had been an all-Asian gathering of churches in John's day, the results would be about the same as in an all-American or world-wide assembly of congregations in our own time. Some of the groups would have everything going right, others would think all was going wrong, and many would relate a conglomeration of examples of faithfulness, conditions of compromise, and cases of evil being tolerated. Whatever their condition, these churches are God's units for carrying out His mission to men. Christ pleads for these communities to "hear what the Spirit says to the churches" (Revelation 2:7). They are His army. To them He entrusted world conquest. They need to remember His order to "disciple the nations." They must recall His promise to be with them "to the very end of the age" (Matthew 28:20). He is shown to be keeping that dependable covenant, for John writes, "I saw seven golden lampstands, and among the lampstands was someone 'like a son of man'" (Revelation 1:12, 13).

C. See the Unveiled Bible

Christians are people of the Book. The Revelation written by John is the grand finale of the sixty-six books that constitute our Bible. One thing it makes evident is the high value New-Covenant Christians place on Old Testament Scriptures.

Many commentaries point out that there are 278 reflections of the Old Testament in the 414 verses of Revelation. A Jesuit scholar, Massyngberde Ford,[4] believes he can find 400 Old Testament allusions. Never is the Jewish Bible quoted formally, but its ideas, its words, its phrases, and its clauses are there in almost every paragraph. It is as if John paints his visions by dipping his pen in Old Testament inkwells.

Paul, as the example of soul-winning across the world, "reasoned ... from the Scriptures, explaining and proving that the Christ had to suffer and rise from the dead" (Acts 17:2, 3). Apollos did the same, "for he vigorously refuted the Jews in public debate, proving from the Scriptures that Jesus was the Christ" (Acts 18:28).

Jesus, the master teacher, had shown His disciples the richness of the ancient Bible when viewed through the eyes of typology. Their hearts burned within them as he "opened the Scriptures." "Beginning with Moses and all the Prophets, he explained to them what was said in all the Scriptures concerning himself" (Luke 24:32, 27).

While, to me, the book in the hand of God that the Lamb will open (Revelation 5) is the book of the future, I can appreciate Otto Piper's insight that the book the Lamb opens is the Old Testament. Princeton's New Testament scholar is aware of the enlarged place the law of Moses and the prophets and psalms had to the believers who came to see that they were written about Christ and fulfilled in Him (Luke 24:44). It is not difficult to see why missionaries go to all the world with a Bible containing Old and New Testaments in hand. What hopes and dreams the Old inspired, the New finds fulfilled in God's Son, who intersected history. Revelation bears out that truth.

---

[4] Anchor Bible Series, Vol. 38 (Garden City, N. Y.: Doubleday, 1975).

D. See the Unveiled Future

It has been raining sermons on Armageddon all over the nation's cities of late. Enter any Bible bookstore, and you soon discover that books on the rapture, the antichrist, or the end of the world sell like hotcakes. We must turn again to Revelation and listen for what God is telling His church. His motive was not to frighten or alarm His people. It was to let His servants know that victory was ahead for them. In the struggles on earth, they needed the perspective of eternity.

When you read a mystery novel, you are aware that in the last chapter you will learn how it all turns out. Revelation is the last chapter. Righteousness will prevail over iniquity. Babylon will be gone, but the holy city will remain forever. The scarlet woman will be no more, but the bride of Christ, "beautifully dressed for her husband" (Revelation 21:2), will abide throughout eternity.

Poets have grasped the confidence this book builds in human hearts as they continue to beat amid the injustices and cruelties of the world:

"Truth, crushed to earth, will rise again;
  The eternal years of God are hers.
But Error, wounded, writhes with pain,
  And dies among his worshippers.[5]

"Right is right, since God is God,
And right the day will win.
To doubt would be disloyalty,
To falter would be sin.[6]

"Never has the tyrant might won the final
    joust with right.
Routed oft and driven back
It has fled before attack.
But when outnumbered one to ten
Right has always struck again.

---

[5] William Cullen Bryant in "The Battlefield" (1839), st. 9. Excerpt quoted in *Bartlett's Familiar Quotations* (Boston: Little, Brown and Co., 1955), p. 471.

[6] F. W. Faber in "The Right Must Win" (1862). Excerpt quoted in J. K. Hoyt: *The Cyclopedia of Practical Quotations* (New York: Funk & Wagnalls Co., 1896), p. 529.

Paradise lost is the opening story of the Bible. Paradise regained is the final chapter.

The "How" Perspective

The slogan, "In essentials unity, in opinions liberty, and in all things charity," is especially appropriate in the study of Revelation. Each follower of Christ may have a strong opinion on how the book should be interpreted. Each Christian has that right. Should my understanding conflict with yours, simply have mercy on my human comprehension. Know that all of Christ's redeemed will share the glories promised no matter how mistaken any brother or sister in the Lord may be.

A discerning question is this: "How are we to look at this Bible book?" In reply, I suggest four words that begin with the letter *D*.

A. The Revelation Is Distinctive

As you read the twenty-two chapters of Revelation, say to yourself, "This Bible book is different from God's inspired message that came to us in the literary form of history or law, for it is apocalyptic in style."

It would be fatal to a right understanding of Scripture to take its history or law sections and allegorize them, as the Gnostics did. That destroys the intended meaning. To take literal writings symbolically is to miss the mark. Conversely, taking symbolic literature literally gets the reader off course as well.

I believe the divinely-given book of Revelation was intended to be taken seriously, but not always literally. The opening verse states that Jesus "sent and signified it by his angel unto his servant John" (Revelation 1:1, ASV). *Signified* suggests signs or symbols will be the form used to convey this message from Heaven. The Revelation communicates to the suffering Christian's feelings, and not exclusively to his rational mind.

The sun's disappearance from view each evening can be explained appropriately in one of two ways. The scientist can give the physical explanation about the earth's rotation. The poet and artist can describe the beauty of the "setting sun." Both forms of expression have their place and are equally true. Revelation comes to us more like a Beethoven symphony that stirs hearts in the music hall than like an Einstein theory designed to challenge keen minds in the lecture room.

At first, do not worry what passages mean. Let them affect you. Be impressed by the colors used (white, red, green, purple, black, and pale-green). Listen to the sound effects (silence, earthquake, thunder, trumpets, harps, winds, and choirs). Say, "God is speaking to all of me—my heart, my longings, my fears, and my feelings—and not just to my brain." This book is distinctive, because it is apocalyptic. When I read of dragons with seven heads and ten horns, I am not to believe there are literal dragons, but I am to know there is a real devil with whose wiles and threats I must deal. Great English literature has place for *Alice in Wonderland* and *Gulliver's Travels*. God, too, can use symbolic literature in getting across His message.

B. *The Revelation Is Dualistic*

We who have trouble with apolyptic literature, finding it alien and strange to our day, need to remember that this literary form was popular in the first century. They knew such literature was symbolic. They further understood that it was dualistic in nature. It visualized the struggle between right and wrong, good and evil, light and darkness.

Biblical apocalyptic was different, however, from Babalonian apocalyptic. In pagan writings, two eternal powers were portrayed in everlasting struggle. They believed in Ahuramazda, the God of Light. They also held the conviction that there was a God of Darkness. This led to a fatalistic view. Holding all things to be cyclical, good would prevail a while, but then evil would take over.

Darkness will not exist forever in Biblical theology. Satan is a created being. As he had a point of beginning, he will have an end. According to Revelation, before the last chapters are over, Satan will be in the lake of fire. He will not be around to cause trouble anymore. The Holy One is almighty and eternal. The dragon and his beasts are defeated. It matters to men that they choose the winning side.

C. *The Revelation Is Deterministic*

From the isle of Patmos comes the last apostle's message. John's fellow apostles have been martyred. His struggling congregations face governmental threats. He is kept from the people he loves by imprisonment for Christ. What will be the outcome? Revelation leaves no doubt, for one of its traits is determinism.

The word *predestination* may properly be used in a Biblical sense. While God did not determine from eternity past that a certain one of His creation would be damned and another should be saved, He did predestine that all who would accept His Son would be sanctified and glorified.

Nothing will stop God from keeping His promise to those in His Son. It is not as if the Redeemer had promised us resurrection, eternal life, and Heaven providing that fifty-one percent of the believers remain true. Neither Christ's coming and our sharing eternity with Him nor Satan's total defeat is based on our measuring up. They are based on Christ's unbreakable promise.

God reveals the future. We read not that this is the way it *may* be *if* man will do his part. We rather are told how it most definitely *will* be. You can count on it! God's eschatology has no room for ifs. Christ will return. Those with garments washed white in the blood of the Lamb will no longer hunger and thirst and shed tears. Their shepherd will guide them to life's waters (Revelation 7:14-17). Where is the mission field where such a promise lacks appeal?

D. The Revelation Is Dramatic

John Wick Bowman's book *The First Christian Drama*[7] presents Revelation not as a made-up story—a fiction—but as a description of events to occur on the stage of world history. After a prelude and before a postlude, Bowman finds seven acts and seven scenes in each of these acts.

The number seven is significant in the Gospel of John, but more outstanding yet in Revelation. Here the number appears forty-four times, to say nothing of the fact that seven beatitudes[8] are scattered throughout the book and twenty-seven different words *(sign,* for instance) are used seven times.

In any drama in the city of Ephesus, there was apt to be a choir before the stage chanting themes to follow in the acts of the play. At the conclusion, the choir of singers would return and let the audience hear the familiar strains again. In the Gospel of John, the prologue (John 1:1-14) and the epilog (John 21:1-25)

---

[7] John Wick Bowman, *The First Christian Drama* (Philadelphia: Westminster Press, 1968).

[8] Revelation 1:3; 14:13; 16:16; 19:9; 20:6; 22:7; 22:14.

served that purpose, as the prologue (Revelation 1:1-3) and the epilog (Revelation 22:6-21) do in Revelation.

We are now ready to take our seats in the theater. The lights are being dimmed. The curtain is rising so we can see each suggested theme acted out. We will be watching for the themes suggested in the key verses of Revelation 1:9, 10. The strains to listen for are about the suffering, the victories, and the steadfastness of those who bear witness to Jesus as they bring the world to sharing in the praise of the Redeemer.

The Perspective of Preaching

CHAPTER ONE

The Perspective of Preaching
"The Word of God and the Testimony of Jesus"

John asserted that he was on the isle of Patmos "because of the word of God and the testimony of Jesus" (Revelation 1:9). He did not mean that the small island was in his long-range plans for spreading the gospel. The facts were quite otherwise. An opposing government had decided that this apostle must be stopped. He was influencing too many of its citizens. He was calling for allegiance to one other than the Caesar. He was preaching that Jesus was Lord. So he was banished to Patmos.

A book that begins with such a statement regarding evangelism (1:9) and concludes with a call for decisions to be made for Christ reveals its intent. The reader cannot escape God's invitation: "The Spirit and the bride say, 'Come!' And let him who hears say, 'Come!' Whoever is thirsty, let him come; and whoever wishes, let him take the free gift of the water of life" (Revelation 22:17). The author did not hide his conviction that the whole church is to be taking the whole gospel to the whole world.

God's World

No provincialist wrote this document. His mind was not mentally confined to the environs of Capernaum or the shore of Galilee. He saw the whole world, even the whole universe. He knew that the Rabbi with whom he walked the roads of Palestine several decades before would extend His reign over land and sea (Revelation 10:2). He wrote, "All nations will come and worship before you" (Revelation 15:4). He reaches out to men of "every nation, tribe, people and language" (Revelation 7:9).

Several times (5:9; 7:9; 10:11; 11:9; 13:7; 14:6; 17:15) we meet these groupings of the human race. There are linguistic groups. There are racial groups. There are clan and blood-related groups. There are national distinctions. Not one segment of humanity is more important than the other. In God's heart, there is abundant room for everyone.

Tribes

Φυλή, the Greek word for *tribe,* is found thirty-one times in the New Testament, twenty-one of which are in Revelation. It has to do with family or blood-related classifications.

Revelation 7:4-8 introduces us to the 144,000 God has sealed from among the twelve tribes. Remember that in the Old Testament, there are twenty listings of these twelve tribes in eighteen different arrangements. Therefore, as we especially meet these tribes now in both chapters 7 and 14 of Revelation, do not give too much care to their arrangement. Rather, observe that there is an equal number from each of the twelve tribes. This says to us, in symbolic language, that God has no special people, no favorite tribe. There is no uniquely blessed tribe from which 140,000 will come into glory with a small number from the remaining groups to total an additional 4,000. Rather, out of every tribe will come converts to the gospel.

This number—144,000—is obtained by squaring the number 12, the number of the tribes of Israel, and multiplying by the cube of 10. This number, said to be "sealed" in chapter 7 (verses 3, 4), are shown to be "redeemed from the earth" in chapter 14 (verse 3). There, significantly, they are termed "firstfruits" (14:4).

The Jewish farmer in Old Testament times would begin his harvest with a swath from some corner of his field. This he would bind together and wave the sheaf before the Lord as the offering of firstfruits. That cutting from the field was not the total harvest, but only the first swath.

I understand John's symbolism to say that already the world harvest of souls had begun. As the book of Acts had recorded, the first swath of Jewish converts had come in numbers like "3,000" (Acts 2:41) then "5,000" (Acts 4:4) then "thousands" (Acts 21:20). John here raised the number to the symbolic 144,000 and added that from beyond the Jewish tribes will come converts from the other nations, tribes, and languages making "a great multitude that no one could count" (Revelation 7:9). What Daniel had prophesied concerning the Messiah's extensive reign (Daniel 7:14), John saw coming to pass.

Nations

Nation ('έθνος) is the word that is the source of our own word *ethnic*. It is also used in the Great Commission as recorded in Matthew 28:18-20. The "ethnics" are to be discipled. They are the people who live together sharing common customs, who constitute a national unity through massing together. *Nations* is the most general of the four words John used.

That the church had done its job in John's vision is clear by the latter part of the book, where John said, "The nations will walk by its light," that is, the light of the Holy city (Revelation 21:24). What the resurrected Jesus assigned, according to Luke's Gospel, the final scenes in Revelation see accomplished: "Repentance and forgiveness of sins . . . preached in his name to all nations" (Luke 24:47). Christ's coming not only made possible the blotting out of sin, it made necessary the blotting out of tribal and national pride. There were to be no super-races, select tribes, or special nations in the church age. Whether one was Jew or Greek, bond or free, male or female mattered not (Galatians 3:28). It was neither hindrance nor help in attaining salvation. That gift was offered freely to all.

Languages

How wonderful was that Pentecost when the church was born! On the heads of the apostles that day were "what seemed to be tongues of fire" (Acts 2:3). These tongues illustrated that it would be by mouth that the gospel story would spread like a flame across the world.

One of the most practical gifts in the first-century church was the gift of tongues or languages. It enabled the church, in its earliest years, to communicate in any language necessary "the wonders of God" (Acts 2:4-11).

Missionaries of the twentieth century find it essential to study diligently in order to acquire the language and dialect of the people to whom they go. But whether one must learn the new tongue or whether the language will be divinely imparted, it is by means of proclamation that the grace of God is made known around the world (Romans 10:17).

Since people congregate in common language groups, God's Word must be translated from the original Hebrew and Greek into words the people can understand. Hence, Revelation is conscious that Heaven's message must get across tribal, national, and linguistic borders. Languages (γλῶσσαι, literally, tongues) are important. John was to consume and digest the angel-sent little book and "prophesy again about many peoples, nations, languages and kings" (Revelation 10:11). The "eternal gospel" was to be proclaimed "to those who live on the earth—to every nation, tribe, language and people" (Revelation 14:6).

People

When John wrote, "People" (λαός), he used a word found 140 times in the New Testament. He was referring to humans of common race or stock or history. The most important question that cries out for an answer is whether God wills for all people to be saved. Certainly the church is meant to be international, intercultural, and multilingual. But can a missionary reach out toward each person of every color, custom, and class, knowing that God wants that individual's salvation? Could the audiences from Ephesus to Laodicea, including any visitors that might be present, take John's words seriously, offering to "whoever wishes, let him take the free gift of the water of life" (Revelation 22:17)?

John's hopeful message, that no one misses the eternal city because of any predetermining on God's part, but only by stubborn rebellion on the man's part, is basic to world evangelism. Does Revelation 22:17 harmonize with the rest of God's revealed truth?

The critical significance of this issue insists on some interpreting of Scripture by Scripture. Begin with Jesus; then hear Paul, Peter, and John. Christ's audience heard the wide appeal, "Come to me, all you who are weary and burdened" (Matthew 11:28). With little children on his lap, Jesus made known God's will regarding every child born (and that would include every one of us): "Your Father in heaven is not willing that any of these little ones should be lost" (Matthew 18:14). Thus saith the Lord also in John 3:16, 17; Luke 7:30; Matthew 23:27; and many other places. The "tares" in the world do not originate in God's will. "An enemy did this" (Matthew 13:28).

To this point—that men with their God-given free will are responsible for their reception or rejection of God's offer of salvation—read Paul (2 Corinthians 5:14, 15; Galatians 3:26-28; Ephesians 2:18, 19; 2 Timothy 4:1-8; Titus 2:11; Acts 17:30, 31), read Peter (2 Peter 3:9; Acts 2:14-21; Acts 10:34), and read John

(Revelation 3:20; 22:17; 1 John 2:1, 2). Then join the voices that call out to all men everywhere: "Come, all you who are thirsty, come to the waters" (Isaiah 55:1). "The Lord . . . is patient with you, not wanting anyone to perish" (2 Peter 3:9).

It is right that this wonderful inclusiveness of God's mercy, reverberating from one end of the Bible to the other, should ring loud and clear in the final writing. No nation is to be left out. No tribal people is to be forgotten. No linguistic group is to fail to have access to God's Word. The Shepherd is searching for His lost sheep. Heaven will break out in joyful praise as each lost one is found (Luke 15:10).

God's Word

The world God wants is the entire world. The word He desires them to hear is the whole gospel. Both of these certainties are affirmed again in Revelation. The church knows *to whom* it is to go. It is to reach "all creation" (Mark 16:15). It also is to understand *with what* message it is to go. It is to declare "the whole will of God" (Acts 20:27). As no person for whom Christ died is to be *left out,* no promise Christ offered is to be *dropped out.*

Man lives by "every word that comes from the mouth of God" (Matthew 4:4). Our assignment is to teach men "to obey everything I [Christ] have commanded" (Matthew 28:20). When God established the old theocracy and gave Israel the Ten Commandments, He did not allow options. His words were not "Here are ten commands, choose any five." In the days of the New Covenant, it would be disloyalty to omit any of the facts or promises or commands. Messengers are responsible to deliver the message as given, without altering it by extension or deletion. The apostles were promised the Holy Spirit's guidance "into all truth" (John 16:13). John showed his faithfulness to that revelation in its totality.

In the early part of Revelation (1:16) and toward the end (19:15), Jesus is pictured as having in his mouth "a sharp double-edged sword" (Revelation 19:15). Just as the dragon has a destructive river of water (lies) flowing from his mouth to reek human destruction (Revelation 12:15), Christ has coming from His lips words of truth that conquer nations. He himself is titled "the Word of God" (Revelation 19:13). He is riding a white horse, the symbol of victory. "The armies of heaven were following him, riding on white horses" (19:14). Their "fine linen, white and clean" is explained as "the righteous acts of the saints" (19:8). My understanding of this imagery is that when the church follows Christ into the world to win it for Him, the words from their lips, backed up with the holiness of their lives, will win the battle.

Old Testament and New Testament

God's written Word, today, is separated into "the witness before the fact" and "the witness after the fact." That is to say, we have the Old Testament and the New Testament.

"His servants the prophets" (Revelation 10:7) are met eight times in Revelation. Since in all but 14 of the 143 times prophets are mentioned in the rest of the New Testament the reference is to Old Testament prophets, it can be assumed that some of the Revelation references are, too.

Speaking of the Old Testament, Jesus said, "You diligently study the Scriptures because you think that by them you possess eternal life. These are the Scriptures that testify about me" (John 5:39). He later spoke of the fulfillment of what was "written about me in the Law of Moses, the Prophets and the Psalms" (Luke 24:44). Peter got his understanding of the purpose of Old Covenant writings from Christ: "The Spirit of Christ in them ... predicted the sufferings of Christ and the glories that would follow" (1 Peter 1:11).

What the ancient prophets said was coming, the recent apostles declared had come. The "twelve apostles of the Lamb" (Revelation 21:14) were foundation stones. As there had been pseudo-prophets of old, there would be false apostles (Revelation 2:2) in the new era. Yet, God's true "apostles and prophets" bear reliable witness to Him. Quite possibly, they are the "two witnesses" of Christ in Revelation 11:3.

This much is generally agreed. The Old Testament prophets gave 333 predictions regarding the Messiah to come. The New Testament apostles gave "Amen!" to the prophet's witness with witness of their own. The Lord, at the ascension, addressed the eleven apostles with the words, "And you will be my witnesses" (Acts 1:8). In their ministries, they affirmed, "We are witnesses of these things" (Acts 5:32). The apostolic author of Revelation also wrote that Jesus' signs were done "in the presence of his disciples" (John 20:30). As the last living apostolic witness, John drew from the rich wells of Old Testament writing, while describing what in vision he had just seen (Revelation 1:11) on the isle of Patmos.

It is this entire Bible that the missionary carries to virgin territory, that the minister carries to the pulpit, and that the Christian carries to his neighbor. Each well knows the distinction between the Old and New Covenants (Hebrews 8:6-9). He is aware that the new wine cannot be held by the old wineskins (Matthew 9:17). But he surely knows one of the most convincing evidences that Jesus is the Messiah is fulfilled prophecy (Acts 17:2, 3). He further finds the ancient stories typical of the experiences the believers share today (1 Corinthians 10:11).

Sweet and Bitter

As Ezekiel before him (Ezekiel 3:1-3), John was invited to take and eat the "little scroll" received from the angel's hand (Revelation 10:8-10). Βιβλαρίδιον is the diminutive for *scroll, book,* or *Bible.* The effects of sweetness and sourness suggest the consequences that flow from God's Word. There are results most sweet from accepting its teaching. There are consequences most dreadful from rejecting its grace. In other words, the sword is two-edged (Revelation 1:16; 2:12, 16). It saves and destroys. It brings redemption and judgment. It offers hope if received and hopelessness if refused—good news and bad news.

The good news of Mark 16:16 is that "whoever believes and is baptized will be saved." The bad news of the same text is that "whoever does not believe will be condemned." One side of Christ's teaching is the gospel that those "born of water and the Spirit . . . enter the kingdom of God" (John 3:5). The other side of the same coin is that "whoever rejects the Son will not see life, for God's wrath remains on him" (John 3:36).

Revelation proclaims the whole gospel. It paints the New Jerusalem in all its glory, where the saints enjoy the presence of their "Maker, Defender, Redeemer, and Friend." It also describes the agony of a lake of fire for those who follow the dragon and bear the mark of the beast. The Jesus of Revelation is consistent in nature with the Jesus of the Gospels. Both grace and judgment are promised by the Lord.[9]

---

[9] Compare just in Matthew: Matthew 8:11-12; 11:5-24; 12:28-32, 38-42; 13:10-17, 24-30, 47 ff; 18:1-9; 25:1-46. The other Gospels could be enlisted to bear like testimony.

John told the truth, the whole truth, and nothing but the truth. We can do no less. "It is required that those who have been given a trust must prove faithful" (1 Corinthians 4:2). All the message from the Old and New Testaments, both the bitter and the sweet, is to be told. How else can the hearers make the right decision? Since the consequence of their choice is eternal, the information leading to the will's action ought to be the whole truth spoken in love (Ephesians 4:15).

Personal and Social

Which Christ is the real Christ? Some more liberal theologians paint a Jesus of social concern—a prophetic voice, like that of Amos, calling for justice to "roll on like a river, [and] righteousness like a never-failing stream" (Amos 5:24). The evangelical thinkers see the message of Jesus relating to personal salvation in words to all, "You must be born again" (John 3:7). The real Jesus of time and eternity cannot be whittled down to the partial gospels of men. He calls for social justice and for personal salvation.

What James, the Lord's half-brother, put in balance in James 1:27, John, one of the Lord's inner-circle disciples, put in equal emphasis in all of Revelation. Visiting "the orphans and widows in their distress" is the right oar. Keeping "oneself from being polluted by the world" is the left oar. No progress can be made without both oars. John, as we shall see, made constant reference to the Lamb's blood that washes stained lives white (Revelation 1:5; 7:14). He likewise reflected God's awareness of the world's injustice. He was not blind to social strife, war, and poverty (Revelation 6). He was not deaf to the cries of victims of murder, adultery, sorcery, and theft (Revelation 8). God knows that some governments keep groups from buying and selling (Revelation 13), while His orderly creation suffers from pollution of every kind (Revelation 16).

Where has Christ's church gone with the gospel without also contributing to improved social conditions? I have found gospel by-products everywhere. Clinics, hospitals, schools, and orphanages dot the hillsides where "soldiers of the cross" have gone. Hungry people have been taught how to get more returns of food from their little plots of land. Sanitary practices have led to longer and more fulfilling lives. Best of all, those learning that they are children of God can accept any kind of bondage to cruel dictators or inhumane land-owners because they know those conditions are only temporary. In Christ, they will be eternally free. The dream of freedom has been planted for patient watering and certain development.

John reminded the redeemed that they are children of the King and no less than priests (Revelation 1:6).

God's Workers

Between the entire world, which God wants reached for His kingdom, and the entire Word, which God wants that world to hear, is the potential "bottle-neck" or the promising "connecting link": the church. John's Revelation shows interest not only in Christ's coming to men (Revelation 1:7), but also in men's coming to Christ (Revelation 22:17). Satan's defeat is attributed to both "the blood of the Lamb" and "the word of their testimony" (Revelation 12:11). Jesus' cleansing blood can be appropriated only by those who hear the saving message. This fact gives preaching high priority (Ephesians 3:10).

Pay attention to the symbols that picture the church from God's viewpoint. Each symbol speaks of believers in their soul-winning ministry. Let me isolate six snapshots of the people of God in this final Bible book.

Martyr

In Revelation 1:1, 2, we meet a martyr (μάρτυς). The Greek word has been translated "witness." Here, John the author is said to be the witness. By verse 5 of the same chapter, Jesus is ascribed "the faithful witness." Later, in Revelation 6:9, we see under an altar large numbers of Christ's disciples who had been slain for the "testimony," or witness, that they held.

Originally, the word μάρτυς only meant witness, but since so many of Christ's witnesses were put to death, the word has evolved to imply dying for one's convictions. Apostles, like John, were witnesses unto death. Jesus witnessed from the Jordan to Calvary. All His followers take up their crosses, aware that beatings go along with the proclamation of the gospel (Mark 13:9, 10).

Missionaries do not go to foreign lands with the gospel because the people of those lands want the Christ, but because the Christ wants the people of those lands. Jesus was the first "foreign" missionary, coming from Heaven to earth. "His own did not receive him" (John 1:11). His witness (μάρτυς) and our witness may be rejected, but all who receive Him are given "the right to become children of God" (John 1:12).

Messenger

Angel ('ἄγγελος) is a common term in the book before us. The translation is "messenger." In some of the seventy-six instances of its use in Revelation, the reference is to Heavenly beings. These "ministering spirits" the Hebrews' author defines as creatures "sent to serve those who will inherit salvation" (Hebrews 1:14). But my personal guess is that the "angel" referred to in association with the individual congregations in Asia (Revelation 1:20; 2:1, 8, 12, 18; 3:1, 7, 14) was the preacher in each case. The postman who delivered the seven letters to the angels of the churches did not seek some extension ladder to reach beyond the clouds, but brought the letters to the appropriate messenger who would read the correspondence to the gathered congregation.

We extend the word *angel* to *evangelist*. Malachi 3:1 predicted a messenger to prepare the Messiah's way. Mark (1:2-4) quoted the passage, using the word 'ἄγγελος. He implied that John the Baptist was the person God had in mind as the prophecy's fulfillment.

The modern church is not misled in using Revelation 14:6, 7 as a fitting text for Reformation Day. "Then I saw another angel flying in midair, and he had the eternal gospel to proclaim to those who live on the earth—to every nation, tribe, language and people." The binding of Satan by an angel in Revelation 20:1, 2 may be read in the light of Paul's observation to the church, "The God of peace will soon crush Satan under your feet" (Romans 16:20).

The message is "the power of God" (Romans 1:16). The messengers ('ἄγγελοι) from Heaven, to bear that message, are the redeemed (Ephesians 3:10). We remember the spirit-being "angel" who guided the preacher to the Ethiopian eunuch (Acts 8:26), but it was the enfleshed "ev*angel*ist" who told the story to the potential convert (Acts 8:35; note Acts 21:8).

Minister

God's church, visualized as martyr and angel (messenger), is also conceptualized as priest or minister. Revelation 1:6 informs the readers that Christ has made them "priests to serve his God and Father." 'Ιερεύς is the Greek word John uses. It is common today to emphasize the Biblical teaching of the priesthood of all believers. That important fact must not be lost for what it implies.

Priests were to be mediators between God and man. They were to speak to God for the people and to speak to the people for God. They were expected to offer sacrificies for the wayward. The New Testament priests knew they were not to continue offering the animal sacrifices of the Old Covenant. Those sacrifices pointed forward to Jesus' perfect sacrifice as "the Lamb of God, who takes away the sin of the world" (John 1:29). The apostles understood that the pleasing sacrifice we can offer to the Father today is a convert. So Paul wrote hoping that "the Gentiles might become an offering acceptable to God" (Romans 15:16). The author of Hebrews called on his readers to "offer to God a sacrifice of praise." This he defined as "the fruit of lips that confess his name" (Hebrews 13:15, 16). To confess Christ before men is our ministry.

The Latin word for *priest* is *pontus*. You remember Roman Catholics refer to their pope as the "Pontifex Maximus," meaning the big bridge. Biblically speaking, every Christian, large or small, is a bridge or priest. Are you seeing yourself as a bridge-builder? You and I are not simply to enjoy the fellowship of believer with believer. We are to build bridges over which the world's present unbelievers may come to their Savior.

Mainstay

The reader of Revelation is to see himself as God sees him. Through Christ's eyes, His disciples are martyrs or witnesses, messengers or angels, ministers or priests, and mainstays or supporters of the truth.

Churches are God's candelabra, lampstands, or candlesticks (Revelation 1:12, 20). Their divinely-given purpose is to uphold the light or the gospel truth. The emphasis is that the congregations exist in communities where darkness abounds. Sin, despair, and ignorance can only be dispelled by the light. Christians have Jesus, "the light of the world" (John 8:12). It is intended that light not be placed "under a bowl," but "on its stand, and it gives light to everyone in the house" (Matthew 5:15).

It is encouraging to note that John saw Jesus walking "among the lampstands" (Revelation 1:13). As long as His congregations are at the task of spreading the gospel, as He assigned, He is with them, as promised (Matthew 28:20).

One of the greatest of all New Testament passages is 1 Timothy 3:16, which is the gospel in a nutshell. Many consider it either an early Christian creed or an early hymn. In the verse that precedes this rythmic review of Jesus' incarnation and victory, the church is called "the pillar and foundation [or mainstay] of the truth." The church is not so much the light as the people upholding the light. John called each congregation a lampstand (λυχνία). The church is not intended to keep its glowing gospel hidden within the walls of its place of assembly. It is to enter the world of darkness and let its light shine.

Militant

What a contrast between the armies of men and the army of God. No pillage or destruction follows where the Christian soldiers march in the name of "the Prince of Peace" (Isaiah 9:6). The army dressed in white following the one called the Word of God, who rode on a white horse, was brought to victory by the sword in His mouth (Revelation 19:11-16).

Christians wear the spiritual armor Paul described in Ephesians 6:10-20. The sword of the Spirit, the helmet of salvation, the shield of faith, and all the rest had been worn by the apostle in his missionary conquests to that point in time. Paul, the special apostle to the Gentile world, said, "The weapons we fight with ... have divine power to demolish strongholds. We demolish arguments and every pretension that sets itself up against the knowledge of God, and we take captive every thought to make it obedient to Christ" (2 Corinthians 10:4, 5).

Jesus, in His earthly ministry, foresaw the future church aggressively entering Satan's domain to set its captives free. He promised that "the gates of Hades will not overcome" that marching body (Matthew 16:18). The purpose of the further "revelation of Jesus Christ" is to record the fall of the devil and all his kingdom. Truth is stronger than error. The light will dispel the darkness. God's army will see the rout of evil. In the end, "The kingdom of the world has become the kingdom of our Lord and of his Christ, and he will reign for ever and ever" (Revelation 11:15).

Mother

As we look at the glorious woman portrayed in Revelation 12, we ask the ancient question of Solomon, "Who is this that appears like the dawn, fair as the moon, bright as the sun, majestic as the stars in procession?" (Song of Solomon 6:10). The scholars' answers differ. To a few, she is Eve, the mother of humanity. Genesis 3:15

proclaimed the "offspring" of the woman would bruise the serpent's head. To a few more she is Mary, the mother of Jesus. Perhaps to most, she is God's bride Israel from which the Messiah came. I lean toward the church, the Bride of Christ, who brings convert after convert into the world. She is said to have as "her offspring" all "those who obey God's commandments and hold to the testimony of Jesus" (Revelation 12:17).

This kind of theology matches apostolic thinking. As Old Covenant Israel was considered Jehovah's bride in the prophets, the New Covenant church was called by the apostles Christ's Bride (Revelation 21:2, 9; Ephesians 5:23-33). Paul considered the Christian espoused "to one husband" (2 Corinthians 11:2), that is, we "belong [are married] . . . to him who was raised from the dead, in order that we might bear fruit to God" (Romans 7:4). That makes all those born again in the age of "regeneration" (Matthew 19:28), when new birth is possible, "children . . . of the free woman" (Galatians 4:31). The Heavenly "Jerusalem . . . is our mother" (Galatians 4:26).

If this conclusion is justified, then the meaning of Revelation 12 could well be that the church, which has been envisioned as a light-bearing institution, a gift-bearing priest, a message-bearing angel, a testimony-bearing witness, and a sword-bearing soldier, is here described as a child-bearing mother.

Just as Satan opposed Jesus, he here spewed floods of lies from his mouth to destroy the church and her converts. The mother's "crown of twelve stars" reminds us that she was first led by the twelve apostles. The "moon" is "under her feet," for she is overcoming the realm of darkness. She is the Lord's chosen entity to bring new life into the world. That is her mission.

The book of Revelation suggested to its readers at the beginning that it would reflect interest in "the word of God and the testimony of Jesus" (Revelation 1:9). Who can hear the chapters that followed without feeling that the whole world lies heavy on the heart of God? Who can read Revelation without recognizing that there is a word of hope extended to that world from the mind of God? And who can view these visions, seen by the apostle, without seeing clearly that the work of the church of God is reaching the world with that Word? "Let the church march on!"[10]

---

[10] "Let the Church March On" by A. H. Ackley. Copyright 1939, Rodeheaver.

The Perspective of Opposition

CHAPTER TWO

The Perspective of Opposition
"Your . . . Companion in the Suffering"

Before you decide which view to hold regarding "the tribulation" of Revelation 4-19[11], put the question on hold while you reread all that the book of Revelation says on the subject. Some Christians speak of themselves as believing in a "pre-tribulation rapture." Others hold to a "mid-tribulation rapture." Still others side with the brethren who think in terms of a "post-tribulation rapture." This is of special interest because the word *rapture* is not in the Bible any more than the words *tribulation* and *seven years* are anywhere combined therein.

The Christians to whom John wrote were fully aware, as are we today, of the sufferings endured by Christ. They were also painfully aware of their own suffering. In that, they were not alone. John made clear in the key verse of his book of Revelation (which we could likewise term his book of Tribulation): "I, John, your brother and companion in the suffering . . ." (Revelation 1:9). Well did John remember that his fellow-apostles had been martyred in their day as the earlier prophets had been in theirs. He also knew what harassment was coming upon the churches to whom he was writing from his place of banishment.

My restudy of the twenty-two chapters of Revelation from the angle of suffering leads me to conclude that there are at least three, and possibly four, great tribulations that John sees. All of them relate to the mission of the church. Each of them we will consider in order.

---

[11]See the appendix at the end of this chapter for a summary of the major views of the "Great Tribulation."

The Great Tribulation of the Lost
(in Gehenna)

The twentieth chapter of our book of study tells of "the lake of burning sulfur" (what earlier versions called "the lake of fire and brimstone," Revelation 20:10). This eternal place of great tribulation for the lost is elsewhere called Hell, or Gehenna. While the word γέεννα is not used in Revelation, it is found twelve times in the New Testament. In eleven of these times, the word came from the lips of Jesus. Most commentaries believe Gehenna, which means Valley of Hinnom, is what John had in mind when he referred six times in Revelation to the lake of fire or of burning sulfur (e.g., Revelation 19:20).

The Bible's teaching on Hell is not a popular theme. We need to face that fact. Many religious writers, from the ancient Clement and Origen to all modern universalists and several popular cults, decry that a God of love would have such a place as Hell for those rejecting His grace. Yet we owe it to ourselves to ask, "What does the Bible say?" and, "What does the Bible mean by what it says?"

Where Hell Is

First, let us look at the symbol and then at what it signifies. Southeast of the walled city of Jerusalem (a type of Heaven) was the city's garbage dump (a type of Hell).

Before the Jews had entered their promised land, the valley of Hinnom had been the center of Molech worship (2 Kings 23:10). The place was also called Topheth (Jeremiah 7:31), which means place of abhorrence or place of burning.

Molech was an iron bull nine feet tall. It was hollow within and contained a roaring fire, kept burning by its priests. Onto the idol's two outstretched and upreaching arms, frightened pagan mothers placed their infants in human sacrifice to this deity. The pagan priests beat drums to drown out the shrieks of the babies, whose lives were supposedly required to appease this angry god.

As the Jews took over the land, they found themselves emotionally unable to build their homes and dwell where such horrible practices could have been performed. They chose rather to make this valley a place fit only for their garbage.

Any day in the time of Jesus, as one looked to the south from the city wall of Jerusalem, he would see smoke rising from the dump. Should a person go there to dig around in the refuse, he would find the worms or maggots eating at the rubbish. (Compare Mark 9:48.) One of the main points Christ made of this refuse heap is that it is "outside" (Revelation 22:15) the holy city. Keep this in mind.

The last two verses of Revelation 20 mention the condition of being apart from God forever. The next thirty-five verses, as one reads into chapters 21 and 22, describe the glories of being with Him eternally in the New Jerusalem. Keep the balance. If you want to know the truth—the whole truth—you need to know God's longing to bring all human beings into the protection and radiance of His holy city. You need also to know that outside, for those refusing to enter, there is the garbage dump.

God's message—even one that comes through symbolism—should be taken very seriously. He does not mislead by exaggeration. Heaven will be better than the physically described city with gates of pearl and streets of gold. Hell will be worse than material fire and worms. To be apart from God and all that is good forever cannot be overstated. Heaven is more wonderful than earthly Jerusalem. Hell is more awful than Gehenna. Both are realities. This awareness ought to keep the church at its mission of rescue.

The city of Revelation 21 is sufficient in size to hold you and yours and everyone else. It is as beautiful as a bride (Revelation 21:2) and as radiant as a gem (Revelation 21:11). No tears will sadden its inhabitants (Revelation 21:4). No "sea" will separate from loved ones (Revelation 21:1). No sirens shall pierce the night as ambulances or hearses take dear ones to hospitals or morgues. There will be no night (Revelation 21:25) or darkness where God is.

What Hell Is

The best definition of Hell I know is separation from God. "Away from me," are Jesus' final words to workers of iniquity (Matthew 7:23). In the parable of the separation of sheep from goats, the King of eternity says, "Depart from me, you who are cursed, into the eternal fire prepared for the devil and his angels" (Matthew 25:41). Paul spoke of Christ's return for ultimate judgment. He used similar words regarding those who "do not obey the gospel of our Lord Jesus," declaring that "they will be punished with everlasting destruction and shut out from the presence of the Lord" (2 Thessalonians 1:8, 9).

Separation from God will be a horrible experience. To be burned would bring dreadful agony. To be in total darkness would be an experience of desperation. To fall down and down endlessly, in a pit without a bottom, is beyond the most grotesque imagination. To be in a garbage dump with the dregs of society—with no relief in sight—is a condition to be abhorred. To be separated from the Light of the world or the Water of life is not God's goodwill for man. Eternal life, rather than the "second death" of eternal separation, is God's preferred option for His creatures. Atonement (at-one-ment), or reconciliation with God, is the blessing offered by those who preach Christ to the world. As the book of Revelation describes the end of Heaven's search for the heart of man, some will be "in" eternity with Him, but some will be "out." Why?

Why Hell Is

Some believe we should take the teaching of Hell out of the Bible. God rather wants to take the experience of Hell out of everyone's future. Hell is the ultimate outcome of God's respect for a human's freedom of choice.

Those who enter glory do so while looking into the face of Christ saying, "Thy will be done!" For God is "not wanting anyone to perish" (2 Peter 3:9). It is His will that we enter Heaven. What is Hell? That is the last resort for God. After every imaginable effort to bring stubborn humans to repentance, but recognizing the free will He has given to men, eventually God must say to those clinging doggedly to their sins, "It is not My will, but *thy* will be done." To transport men on earth, as they are, to some other locale high above the earth would not make it Heaven. Heaven, without Hell, is an impossibility. There ultimately must be a separation of those who will to do God's will and those who rebel against it.

Man must either be a robot who will be forced to do what the Creator wills, or he must be free to be a creature in God's image, able to make choices. Those who go into all the world to preach the gospel cannot force people to make the decision the messengers and their Christ would prefer. But they can tell the whole message of God so their hearers can make their own decision in the light of all the facts.

There is "great tribulation" for the lost revealed in Revelation. It is an eternal tribulation. Before we consider the other great tribulations referred to in this book, ask one more question regarding the eternally damned in Gehenna. When shall it begin?

When Hell Is

The extensive description John has given of Heaven and Hell in his final chapters has prepared the reader to respond to the concluding appeal for a right choice: "Come ... take the free gift of the water of life" (Revelation 22:17). John informed our minds by letters dictated, by a book being opened, by trumpets sounding, and by bitter happenings experienced. All of the prior divine efforts are to help us make the choice in time that will save us from the final catastrophe in eternity. Hell is the last resort, when there is no more that God can do for the people He made.

We are told that Hell is "forever" and has no end, and that it is "day and night," knowing no intermission. Such descriptive material is given not just so the mind can be informed, but so the will can be spurred to act. "To be or not to be" is not the question. It is rather, "To be with God or without God," endlessly. "So it will be at the end of the age" (Matthew 13:40). Revelation 14:14-16 pictures the righteous lovingly harvested and 14:17-20 describes the evil totally crushed.

We have a job to do. History has not concluded yet. That is the reason the church, throughout all the time remaining on earth, must emphasize evangelism and missions.

The Great Tribulation of the Lamb
(on Golgotha)

One great tribulation, the greatest tribulation of all, is in the eternity yet to come. To keep that tribulation from happening to all, another great tribulation occurred in history. It is mentioned throughout the book of Revelation. This tribulation took place not in Gehenna, but on Golgotha. Reading Revelation, the student is impressed with the great suffering awaiting the lost, those who refuse to accept God's grace. He is likewise reminded of the great suffering God's Lamb underwent to offer that grace, to make possible deliverance from eternal judgment.

Jesus is symbolically called the "Lamb" approximately

twenty-eight times,[12] because His sacrifice for sins is in the forefront of all gospel preaching. His blood was said to redeem (Revelation 1:5; 5:9), cleanse (7:14; 19:13), and overcome (12:11). His death (1:18; 2:8) or slaying (5:6, 9; 13:8) was by piercing (1:7), or crucifixion (11:8). The Lamb made war with the dragon, not by killing others, but by dying himself. Christ's followers are not overcome by the size of bombs the enemy can stockpile, but the enemy is overcome "by the blood of the Lamb" (Revelation 12:11). The robes of the redeemed have been "washed" and "made . . . white in the blood of the Lamb" (Revelation 7:14).

The cross is the central fact of divine revelation. "Paradise lost" becomes "Paradise regained" because of Calvary. To open the Bible anywhere is to read about the blood-sprinkled way of the cross. The Old Testament, in the types of the Law (like the sacrifice of Isaac), in the teaching of the Prophets (e.g., Isaiah 53), or the tenor of the Psalms (e.g., Psalm 22), "predicted the sufferings of Christ" (1 Peter 1:11). For centuries of time, spotless lambs were put to death vicariously for guilty men, until God's perfect Lamb had come. "Christ died for our sins according to the Scriptures" (1 Corinthians 15:3).

The New Testament Gospels are often called by the scholars "passion narratives." The point is that they are not attempts at biography. They are sermons centering on the sacrificial death of Jesus, who came "to give his life as a ransom for many" (Mark 10:45). The Gospel of John, for example, contains twenty-one chapters and by its twelfth chapter has you in the last week of Jesus' life. The first part of this and the other Gospels is to inform you who the Son of Mary is. The rest of the message is that He died and rose again for your sins. C. H. Dodd, in his *Apostolic Preaching,*[13] demonstrates that the missionary sermons in Acts proclaim the same saving facts that the written Gospels herald. Even though the epistles were written to persons

---

[12] Revelation 5:6, 8, 12, 13; 6:1, 16; 7:10, 17; 12:11; 13:8; 14:1, 4, 10; 15:3; 17:14; 19:7; 21:9, 22, 23, 27; 22:1, 3.

[13] C. H. Dodd, *Apostolic Preaching and Its Developments: Three Lectures with an Appendix on Eschatology and History* (Grand Rapids: Baker, 1980).

already "under the blood," having accepted the substitutionary sacrifice of Christ, they call the readers' minds back to the story they must never forget. Recall the familiar excerpts of Paul (1 Corinthians 1:27; 15:3; Philippians 2:5) and John (1 John 1:7). Now add the constant echoing of the familiar truth about Jesus' suffering in Revelation. The sum of the matter is that all the Bible, in all its parts including Revelation, tells the same story.

The ordinances Christ gave His church preach the same gospel. We are "baptized into his death" (Romans 6:3) to begin our lives in Christ. We continue reminding ourselves of the price of our redemption at the regular worship of the church, where in the Lord's Supper, we "proclaim the Lord's death until he comes" (1 Corinthians 11:26).

Walk through cemeteries lined with crosses. Visit the art galleries and note the crucifixion scenes. Look at books on church architecture or listen to the hymns of the centuries. Much of what you see and hear was inspired by the symbolism of Revelation and all the Biblical writings that preceded it. The church has a story to tell to the nations. God's Son came from eternity into time to go through the tribulation of Golgotha so that men need not suffer the tribulation of Gehenna. The suffering of the Lamb makes unnecessary the suffering of the lost. To be found, rather than lost, man need only to hear and respond to the gospel message.

The Great Tribulation of the Laborers
(Across the Globe)

We know there will be tribulation in eternity for the lost. We also know about Jesus' taking on mortality so He could suffer tribulation and die for the world on Calvary. What we would now like to discover is what tribulation is to befall the church. Revelation attributes victory to "the blood of the Lamb and ... the word of their testimony; they did not love their lives so much as to shrink from death" (Revelation 12:11). This book tells of "the souls of those who had been slain because of the word of God" (Revelation 6:9), even "beheaded because of their testimony for Jesus" (Revelation 20:4).

The key verse of Revelation 1:9 began, "I, John, your brother and companion in the suffering...." John was not foreseeing a tribulation two thousand years in the future. He was sharing in one at the very time of his visions. Θλίψις, the word he uses, was usually translated "tribulation" in older versions, although the NIV so translates it only once (Revelation 7:14). It could also be translated "ordeal" or "affliction." Originally, the word was used to describe the pressure, the crushing, pinching, or squeezing, that occurred when grapes were trampled or pressed together to obtain wine.

John's faithfulness to his mission had brought banishment. Scourgings, fetters, scanty clothing, insufficient food, loneliness, and weariness accompanied the darkness of his prison and the dampness of the bare ground on which he likely slept. But he knew that such a lot went with proclaiming the Christ of the cross. He envisioned what the others were facing as they bore testimony to Jesus. He mentioned "tribulation" (1:9; 2:9, 10; 7:14; even though the NIV uses four different words—suffering, affliction, persecution, and tribulation—John used the same Greek word in each of these references), "poverty" (2:9), "suffering," "prison" and "testing" (2:10). He spoke of his coworkers' being "slain" and "killed" (2:13; 6:9, 11; 13:10, 15; 17:6) like animals sacrificed on an altar (6:9). Five times he told of their "blood" being spilled (6:10; 16:6; 17:6; 18:24; 19:2). He knew of their "hunger" and "thirst" (7:16), and their "tears" (7:17; 21:4). He felt their "mourning," "crying," and "pain" (21:4), and their "bitter" lot (10:9). He described them as "trampled" under foot (11:2) and "clothed in sackcloth" (11:3). They were "harmed" (11:5) and "gloated over" by their enemies (11:10). They were "accused" (12:10), "pursued" (12:13) and "swept away" (12:15). They brought into the world a message of love only to receive "rage" (12:17) and to face "war" (12:17; 13:4, 7) resulting in "death" (11:9; 12:11; 14:13). Yet, without such heroic "labor" (14:13) to get the message out, Christ would have died in vain.

The church has understood its order to preach the good news to every creature. Jesus "for the joy set before him endured the cross, scorning its shame" (Hebrews 12:2). His servants are to know that, by comparison with the unending happiness of eternity, their suffering will last but "ten days" (2:10). The same devil behind Christ's persecution is behind what the church is facing. Let the church remember, in the heat of the battle, that such tribulation from Satan is the final convulsions of a conquered foe.

Some nonsymbolic writings in the New Testament will help us grasp Revelation's teaching on the suffering the Christian is to face. Thumb through your Gospels, and note how clear Jesus was in telling His followers what to expect. In Matthew we hear, "Blessed are you when people insult you, persecute you and falsely say all kinds of evil against you because of me" (Matthew 5:11). "They will hand you over to the local councils and flog you in their synagogues. On my account you will be brought before governors and kings as witnesses to them and to the Gentiles" (Matthew 10:17, 18). "Do not be afraid of those who kill the body" (Matthew 10:28). According to Matthew, Jesus foresaw His servants during the entire church age hungry, thirsty, naked, and in prison (Matthew 25:42, 43). This conflicts sharply with some modern preaching that promises economic betterment as one certain result of following the Master.

In Mark, Jesus said He came "to serve, and to give his life as a ransom for many" (Mark 10:45). In pursuit of Christlikeness, the Christian will, for the sake of redeeming the lost, "suffer many things and be rejected ... and ... be killed" (Mark 8:31). Jesus warned in Luke's Gospel that being His disciple included following His teaching that "anyone who does not carry his cross ... cannot be my disciple" (Luke 14:27). John's Gospel has the same message: "The man who loves his life will lose it, while the man who hates his life in this world will keep it for eternal life" (John 12:25). Let the believer remember, in the thick of the battle, that his Lord said, "If the world hates you, keep in mind that it hated me first. If you belonged to the world, it would love you as its own. As it is, you do not belong to the world, but I have chosen you out of the world. That is why the world hates you" (John 15:18, 19). If any false ideas still remained about earthly thrones in an earthly kingdom for Jesus' followers, He dispelled them all when he reached the bottom line, "In this world you will have trouble [tribulation]. But take heart! I have overcome the world" (John 16:33).

The history book of Acts proudly tells the story of Stephen, the first Christian martyr (Acts 6:8—7:60). It records the account of James, the first apostle to be put to death for his witness (Acts 12:2). It relates Christ's call to Saul of Tarsus, who had done much "harm" to the saints (Acts 9:13; 22:4), informing him "how much he must suffer" (Acts 9:16). As all the church rejoiced "because they had been counted worthy of suffering disgrace for the Name" (Acts 5:41), so Paul was soon preaching that "we must go through many hardships [tribulations] to enter the kingdom of God" (Acts 14:22).

This reading of texts from the Gospels and Acts may seem long, but we must push on into the epistles. The message is important to understanding the book of Revelation and the lot you may have in the world. It may not be an easy one here, but "great is your reward in heaven" (Matthew 5:12). If life is luxuriant for you, you may well ask if you are making a sufficient sacrifice in supporting the spread of the gospel. Many a missionary has sacrificed his health, if not his life, in getting the message into new areas.

In Romans, Paul wrote of rejoicing not only "in the hope of the glory of God," but also "in our sufferings" (Romans 5:2, 3). He honestly could say, "I consider that our present sufferings are not worth comparing with the glory that will be revealed in us" (Romans 8:18). Could "trouble or hardship or persecution or famine or nakedness or danger or sword" discourage those of whom it was written, "For your sake we face death all day long"? Paul's triumphant cry in the face of all Satan could hurl against him was, "No, in all these things we are more than conquerors through him who loved us" (Romans 8:35-37). William Hendriksen, finding that the teaching of the epistles throws light on the correct understanding of Revelation, used Paul's phrase "More Than Conquerors" as the title for his exceptional commentary on Revelation (Grand Rapids: Baker, 1940).

Since Christ's followers are apt to meet stiff opposition in their proclamation of the gospel, Paul declared, "If only for this life we have hope in Christ, we are to be pitied more than all men" (1 Corinthians 15:19). A good decade before his ministry for Christ ended in beheading at Rome, Paul could list abundant labors, prisons, stripes, beatings with rods, stonings, shipwrecks and other perils that had already befallen him (2 Corinthians 11:23-28). His body showed "the marks of Jesus" (Galatians 6:17). Several of his letters were written from imprisonment. He knew what he labeled "the fellowship of sharing in [Christ's] sufferings" (Philippians 3:10). In his final letter, he predicted for the church "terrible times" (2 Timothy 3:1), stating that "everyone who wants to live a godly life in Christ Jesus will be persecuted" (3:12). He himself was "already being poured out like a drink offering" (4:6; note Numbers 15:1-10).[14]

To continue reading in Hebrews (10:32-34; 12:4) or James (1:2-4) or Peter (1 Peter 1:6, 7; 2:21-23; 4:12-19; 5:8, 9), one rightly draws the conclusion that it is dangerous to be a follower of Jesus. It takes courage to join in taking the gospel message into Satan's territory. The river of water from the serpent's mouth is meant to destroy the woman and "her offspring—those who obey God's commandments and hold to the testimony of Jesus" (Revelation 12:16, 17).

God, who could have kept Daniel out of the lion's den and his three friends out of the fiery furnace in the first place, did not. The Almighty Creator, who could have protected John from banishment on Patmos and Antipas his "faithful witness" from death (Revelation 2:13) chose not. He who knows that flowers spread beautiful aromas when crushed, that gold is purified in the fire, finds evidence of sincere love for the lost when self giving is the price gladly paid.

Let the laborers for Christ across the globe and across the centuries remember that after the cross is the crown. After the tribulation is the triumph. The saved with Christ, wearing the "white robes" of justification and bearing in their hands the "palm branches" of victory, have "come out of the great tribulation" (Revelation 7:9-14) that the world has brought against them. That this reference has to do, not with a few at one period of Christian history, but with all those who have served Christ across the centuries is evident by the description of the eternal state of all the saved. They "serve him [God] day and night," knowing neither hunger or thirst or tears, for the Lamb is "their shepherd" (Revelation 7:15-17).

The Great Tribulation at the Last
(Under Gog)

Now we move from solid ground to the less substantial. We step from the clear to the more debatable. Opinions vary widely when the topic turns from general opposition against the church

---

[14]Also compare Romans 12:12; 1 Corinthians 4:8-13; 7:26; 2 Corinthians 4:17; Ephesians 3:13; 5:16; Philippians 1:20, 21; Colossians 1:24; 1 Thessalonians 1:6; 2:14, 15; 3:2-5; 2 Thessalonians 1:6, 7; 2:8.

across the centuries to discussion of a particular intensified "tribulation" believed by many to precede the millennium of Revelation 20.

Do the volumes of books written and the myriads of sermons preached on a coming great tribulation have a portion of truth behind them? In addition to the total tribulation awaiting the lost in eternity and the intense tribulation Jesus underwent on Golgotha and the centuries of tribulation that have come against the church in its effort to get the gospel out, is there yet in the future a special period to be denoted "the Great Tribulation"?

Imagine, if you will, several large question marks, and in their midst a gigantic exclamation point. That will illustrate both my dilemma and my certainty. As I read the volumes describing a future "great tribulation" and an accompanying "rapture," I am left with many honest questions unsatisfied. But one fact—the certainty of ultimate victory for the church—is undisturbed, whichever view on the other issue proves to be right.

Walk with me for a few moments from the book of Revelation to a few distant passages where some brothers find their information to interpret such passages as Revelation 7:14. We are asked to turn to the book of Daniel and, especially, to Jesus' apocalyptic discourse in Matthew 24, Mark 13, and Luke 21, where our Lord spoke of "'the abomination that causes desolation,' spoken of through the prophet Daniel" (Matthew 24:15). Jesus added, "Then there will be great distress, unequaled from the beginning of the world until now—and never to be equaled again" (Matthew 24:21).

Instead of that prediction awaiting fulfillment, the foretold tribulation was that suffered by the Jewish nation that had rejected their messiah (Matthew 23:37, 38) when their temple was destroyed (Matthew 24:1, 2) in that very "generation" (Matthew 24:34).

History tells us that in A.D. 70, Titus and his army "surrounded" Jerusalem and "its desolation" was "near" (cf. Luke 21:20). This was not only Jesus' interpretation of Daniel, but also that of the Jewish historian of the time. Josephus, in *Antiquities* X.ii.7 and in *Wars* VII, calls A.D. 70 the fulfillment of Daniel's prophecy of the "abomination of desolation." In that siege, 1,100,000 Jews perished and 97,000 were taken captive. The disciples of Jesus understood Him to have been speaking to them of an event to happen in their day. Seeing the signal of the holy land and the holy city surrounded by armies, they fled as instructed, avoiding the desolation. Eusebius says they escaped to Pella.

This war of Rome against Jerusalem was declared by Vespasian in February of A.D. 67 and concluded with the city's fall in August of 70, totalling three and a half years. The earlier enemy of Israel, Antiochus IV of Syria (Antiochus Epiphanes), had warred against the Jews from June 168 B.C. to December 165 B.C., another three-and-a-half-year period of suffering. Judas Maccabaeus succeeded in resisting Antiochus' efforts to hellenize Jewish culture, though he failed to stop him from placing an altar to Zeus in the temple. Hanukkah (the feast of dedication) is the Jewish festival that, to this day, reminds Jews of the price paid to restore the temple. John, in Revelation, may be drawing on these historical instances of recent memory for his three and a half years, "time, times and half a time" (12:14), "42 months" (11:2; 13:5), and "1260 days" (11:3). The fleeing to "the wilderness" (Revelation 12:6) could be suggestive of the disciples' flight toward Pella.

Do you see why question marks are in my mind? There was Antiochus Ephiphanes. There was Titus. In John's day, there was Domitian. But must there be another "beast" yet to arise before history concludes? The "antichrists" of 1 and 2 John (1 John 2:18, 22; 4:3; 2 John 7) may be references to the Gnostics. The "man of sin" of 2 Thessalonians was thought by many protestants to refer to "the papacy" to arise when pagan Rome fell. Will there be another "beast"? Many Christians think so. But, at the same time, a number think not so.

Let me tell you what we all know. Christ will win, and hence all that are on His side will be the victors. To be saved, I need not know who the antichrist is, but who Christ is. I may not know in detail *what* is coming, but I know *Who* is coming. To be among the redeemed, it is not required that one be right on Revelation, but that one be right with God. I place my exclamation point not on knowing the meaning of 666, but on knowing the meaning of life in Christ.

Satan is going to meet his "Armageddon" (Revelation 16:16). There may or may not be other antichrists. There may or may not be further tribulations ahead. But this much is certain: trials and sufferings for the people of God are not the end of the story. Egyptian bondage was not the end of the story. Babylonian exile was not the end of the story. The crucifixion of Jesus was not the end of the story. What is the end of the story for the suffering church? The answer to that is wrapped up in the word Armageddon.

Literally, the Hebrew word *Armageddon* means Mount Megiddo. The Old Testament knows a valley or plain by the name "Megiddo." The nearest mountain was Mount Carmel where Elijah defeated the prophets of Baal (1 Kings 18). In the plain of Megiddo, the Israelite army, though often outnumbered, won the victory by God's intervention.

At Megiddo, the Canaanites under Jabin and Sisera met defeat at the hands of Deborah and Barak (Judges 4, 5). At Megiddo, the Midianites lost to Gideon (Judges 7:1).

What meeting one's "Waterloo" has meant since the time of Napoleon's defeat, meeting one's "Armageddon" has meant since Old Testament days. The word has become a signal of certain defeat for evil by the hand of God. I believe John was suggesting to the church in tribulation that they can look forward to Christ's return when all remaining enemies will be defeated. "Armageddon," like "Gehenna," is a symbol. All the world's lost would not fit in the literal Valley of Hinnom, and all the gathered world's armies could not be contained in the literal Megiddo.

I expect no extended battle between earthly nations. Armageddon is the climactic battle between Satan's forces and those of Christ. It is not a long battle with one side predominating and then another. Revelation does not describe the battle, only its outcome. Christ will appear and "overthrow [the lawless one] with the breath of his mouth and destroy [him] by the splendor of his coming" (2 Thessalonians 2:8). This sounds so much like Christ. He simply spoke a word to the fig tree which promised fruit but supplied none, and it withered away. The raging storm on the sea of Galilee heard His one word *shalom* or *peace,* and perfect calm was restored. At creation, He uttered, "Let there be light," and there was light. So, as to the devil, when Christ comes back, "one little word shall fell him."

Martin Luther read the book of Revelation and reflects it in his hymn, *"Ein' Feste Burg":*

> A mighty fortress is our God,
>   A bulwark never failing;
> Our helper He, amid the flood
>   Of mortal ills prevailing:
>
> For still our ancient foe
>   Doth seek to work us woe;
> His craft and power are great,
>   And, armed with cruel hate,
> On earth is not his equal.
>
> Did we in our own strength confide,
>   Our striving would be losing,
> Were not the right Man on our side,
>   The man of God's own choosing:
>
> Dost ask who that may be?
>   Christ Jesus, it is He;
> Lord Sabaoth His name,
>   From age to age the same,
> And He must win the battle.
>
> The Prince of Darkness grim,
>   We tremble not for him;
> His rage we can endure,
>   For lo, his doom is sure;
> *One little word shall fell him.* [15]

It will be helpful to remember that the battle with Gog and Magog follows the millennium of Revelation 20. At the end of the thousand years, during which Satan has been restricted in his efforts to stop the church's missionary advance, he marshalls all his cohorts in a final thrust. Rather than their being particular nations, they are apt to be atheism, humanism, communism, materialism, hedonism, alcoholism, and every form of corrupt religion and practice. John's progress of thought from the vision of Christ (chapter 1), message to the congregations (2, 3), judgments on enemies (4-19), the kingdom (20:1-6), the attack of Gog (20:7-10), and final glory in the new Jerusalem may be

---

[15] Martin Luther, "Ein' Feste Burg"; tr. by Frederick H. Hedge, "A Mighty Fortress Is Our God," stanzas 1, 2, 3b. Italics mine.

based on Ezekiel's outline of the vision of God (chapter 1), message to the Jews (2-24), judgment on the nations (25-32), the Messianic kingdom (33-37), the attack of Gog (38-39), and final glory (40-48).

I lean toward viewing "Gog and Magog" as symbols for the darkness and the realm of darkness, which shall end. I do not know when Christ is coming, but I do know that when He comes, history will turn out right. Jesus' promise to "come soon," or suddenly (Revelation 22:12), did not assure an immediate return. It rather suggested that when the unrevealed time (Matthew 25:13) happened, it would happen suddenly and unexpectedly like the coming of a "thief" (1 Thessalonians 5:2). Until that climactic day, let the church labor at the work assigned. Should we fall in the battle to evangelize the world, we shall go with the others, in blood-washed robes, to the land of perfect peace, from "the great tribulation" that was ours in the world (Revelation 7:14).

APPENDIX

Views on the Great Tribulation

Revelation 7:14 identifies a great multitude of white-robed saints in Heaven as those "who have come out of the great tribulation." Who are these saints, and what is the nature of the tribulation they have endured?

The answers given to that question are many and varied. The easiest way to survey the most popular answers is perhaps to link them with the millennial theories with which they are commonly associated.

Premillennial Theories

Premillennialists believe in a literal one-thousand-year earthly reign of Christ. They can be divided into pretribulationists, midtribulationists, and posttribulationists.

Pretribulationists believe that Christians will not endure the Great Tribulation. Instead, Christ will rapture the church out of the world before its onset. The Great Tribulation then extends from the rapture to the battle of Armagedon and the establishment of Christ's millennial kingdom. It is a seven-year period when "the unsaved will suffer from intense divine judgments, Israel will be persecuted severely, and saved Gentiles will suffer martyrdom" (Floyd H. Barackman, *Practical Christian Theology* [Old Tappan: Revell, 1981, 1984], p. 348).

"*Posttribulationists* see the Church continuing on earth to the end of the tribulation when the rapture occurs." (G. R. Lewis, "Tribulation," *Zondervan Pictorial Encyclopedia of the Bible* [Grand Rapids: Zondervan, 1975, 1976], p. 820). According to their view, Christians will endure the Great Tribulation, which, for their sake, will be shortened (Matthew 24:22). Then the Lord will return and set up His millennial kingdom.

Midtribulationists combine the two previous theories. They believe the church will endure the first half of the Great Tribulation, but will then be raptured. The world will continue in even more severe tribulation until the second coming.

Postmillennial Theory

Postmillennialists believe the millennium will be a golden age of the church. They believe the efforts of the church will "bind Satan" and so improve the state of the world that Christ can be said to be reigning on earth through the church for a thousand years. At the end of the thousand years, when Satan is released (Revelation 20:7), comes the Great Tribulation. This period will continue until Christ returns and the Judgment Day occurs.

Amillennial Theory

Amillennialists believe the church age is the millennium. The thousand years are figurative for a long time—or, perhaps, a complete time, a time that completes God's plan. The Great Tribulation is a continuation—although perhaps intensified as the second coming approaches—of the tribulation already being suffered by Christians. In this view, only Christians will endure the Great Tribulation, for it is a filling up of the sufferings of Christ (Colossians 1:24). The persecuted will be vindicated when Christ returns and judges the world. (See Θλίψις in Kittel, *Theological Dictionary of the New Testament* [Grand Rapids: Eerdmans, 1965], pp. 139-148.)

The Perspective of Advance

CHAPTER THREE

The Perspective of Advance
"Your ... Companion in the ... Kingdom"

I like books that have happy endings, where "they all lived happily ever after." The book of Revelation is the happy ending of God's Bible. It has, indeed, spoken of the conflict and opposition that the church will meet in carrying out its mission. But it leaves no doubt that Satan's onslaught will fail. The gospel will advance. At the end, Christ will come back "with the clouds, and every eye will see him" (Revelation 1:7). The final words of Jesus in the book are, "Yes, I am coming soon." And the human response is, "Amen. Come, Lord Jesus" (Revelation 22:20).

Jesus himself is responsible for the blessed hope in the heart of His church. He promised His disciples, "I will come back and take you to be with me" (John 14:3). Angels confirmed the promise at His ascension, assuring Jesus' followers, "This same Jesus, who has been taken from you into heaven, will come back in the same way you have seen him go into heaven" (Acts 1:11). As the high priest of the Old Testament went beyond the veil of the temple into the holy of holies and then would return again into view, Jesus would "appear a second time ... to bring salvation to those who are waiting for him" (Hebrews 9:28). The church creeds and the church hymns across the centuries have expressed this common hope of all Christians. Jesus will return! With united voices, the church professes agreement regarding the second coming.

Then comes Revelation 20, and the oneness shatters. The ranks divide as to when Christ will return in relation to the thousand years mentioned there. Some believers claim to be premillennialists, others postmillennialists, and still others amillennialists. More segmentation sets in with camps forming for those holding to a pretribulation rapture, or a midtribulation rapture, or a posttribulation rapture. On nothing are Christians (including the Evangelicals) more divided than in their views of Revelation 20. Here, alone, in all the Bible, we meet the millennium. All the texts on the second coming in the previous Bible books (even in the previous nineteen chapters of this book) must be reinterpreted in the light of these few verses.

Some condensed definitions are in order. What is a premillennialist? The term implies that Jesus' return will be prior to the thousand years of Revelation 20. The premillennialist understands the kingdom mentioned to be an earthly reign of Christ that will be established at His coming. This was a widely held view from Papias to Tertullian. A recent premillennial opinion, called Dispensationalism, has reinterpreted the premillennial view. It was invented by Darby and popularized by Scofield. It is heralded today by Lindsay, Walvoord, Pentecost, and others.

A postmillennialist anticipates the return of Jesus only after a utopian condition of a thousand years has been brought about, in consequence of gospel preaching across the globe.

An amillennialist expects no millennium. The "a," or "alpha," in Greek, is a negative. If a "theist" is a believer in God, the word "atheist" speaks of one who believes there is no God. Where a "Gnostic" is one who says, "I know," an "agnostic" says, "I do not know." So a "millennialist" looks for a literal thousand years of time, while an "amillennialist" does not. You ask how can an amillennialist deny the thousand years, since it is so certainly mentioned in the chapter before us? How could a major portion of the church for all the centuries, since Augustine's *City of God,* hold such a view? Indeed, how does the modern Missouri Synod Lutheran Church, the Orthodox Presbyterian Church, or the Church of God make this their official position today? What caused giants of the faith, like Jonathan Edwards or Matthew Henry, to think in these terms? These brothers did not erase Revelation 20 from their Bibles, but rather thought that, if the rest of the book was symbolic, so would be the "thousand years." Amillennialists understand the "thousand years" to refer to the long, indeterminate period of time the church carries on its missionary task.

Please feel no pressure to accept any particular opinion on this topic. But understand that all the saved, no matter how mistaken their notions, will share in every good God has in mind for His own. An objective understanding of a different view from one's own will contribute to healthy brotherly relations. My views have certainly changed over the years. I invite you to consider some thoughts that have brought me to where I stand as of this moment.

Four questions I raise: (1) "Has a key been found?" (2) "Has the Lord been crowned?" (This asks whether Christ is King or is yet to become King.) (3) "Did a trumpet sound?" (Here we need to inquire whether all resurrections of the Bible are future.) (4) "Has the Devil been bound?" (This last query has stimulated some to joke that, if he has, it certainly has been with a long rope.)

Has a Key Been Found?

Ten times ten times ten is a thousand. Could such a number be considered symbolic in a symbolic book? Certain Bible interpreters call for taking most all of the Bible literally. Every Christian takes all parts of God's revealed Word seriously, but some question if God intended every word of it to be taken literally. They see God using a variety of literary forms in making His will known to men.

We read that God "turned His back" or "wrote with His finger" or shelters us "under His wing." We get the vital spiritual message without insisting our heavenly Father has feathers, knuckles, or a backbone. That would make the need for the incarnation superfluous (John 1:18). "God is Spirit," taught Jesus (John 4:24). He is "invisible," wrote Paul (1 Timothy 1:17), adding ". . . whom no one has seen or can see" (1 Timothy 6:16).

We can share the joy of Isaiah without insisting that, literally, "the mountains and hills will burst into song . . . and all the trees of the field will clap their hands" (Isaiah 55:12). We can gain insight from aged Jacob's words to his sons, without limiting him to using only literal terminology. Was Judah in a literal sense "a lion's cub" (Genesis 49:9), or Benjamin "a ravenous wolf" (Genesis 49:27)? Then, certainly, in apocalyptic literature, Jesus does not of necessity have to be on a "horse" or with "a sword in his mouth," when He returns. A book of "frogs" and "dragons" may well have time lengths with other than literal meanings.

One thousand in certain contexts may only be indicating large numbers. In Revelation 20, it may be indicating many years. God owns "the cattle on a thousand hills" (Psalm 50:10). The

Psalmist assures those who trust in God: "A thousand may fall at your side" (Psalm 91:7). Job reminds the "know-it-all" that in contention with God, "he could not answer him one time out of a thousand" (Job 9:3). Jehovah keeps His covenant "to a thousand generations" (Deuteronomy 7:9). Maybe you remember your mother urging you as a child to brush your teeth, possibly adding, "I've told you a thousand times." Surely Peter, as David before him, was using "a thousand years" to mean a long, long time, when he wrote, "With the Lord a day is like a thousand years, and a thousand years are like a day" (2 Peter 3:8; Psalm 90:4).

We must interpret the Bible by the Bible. How long will Jesus reign according to the Old Testament prophets? "Forever" is the word used by Daniel (Daniel 2:44). He foresaw the Messiah's receiving "an everlasting dominion" (Daniel 7:14). How long will God's Son rule according to other portions of the prophecy in Revelation? "He will reign for ever and ever" (Revelation 11:15) are the words that precede chapter 20. They remain the words that follow chapter 20 (Revelation 22:5).

What, then, is the thousand years? Do they not symbolize the indefinite but lengthy church age, of whatever length that may be? Will we reign with Jesus a thousand years, or will we reign with him forever? Both! The former words refer to the church militant, the latter to the church triumphant. At the consummation of the age, Christ's rule will go on into eternity.

One does himself a favor by realizing that in a cyclical book that takes the reader from John's day to the end of time, the events in chapter 19 may not chronologically precede the happenings of chapter 20. Rather, they may be different ways of viewing the same scenes.

It will be helpful to note what is not mentioned in the troubling passage of Revelation 20. Often our thoughts have been preconditioned by extrabiblical literature on the subject. If the "Jew," or "Jerusalem," or the "land of Palestine" is in chapter 20, it is in invisible ink. No translation or Greek text mentions a literal "throne of David" or the "conversion of the Jewish nation." It rather suggests that even before Satan's demolition in the lake of fire, he is limited in his deception of the nations. Those he has martyred in their testimony for Christ will, in some sense, "reign" in victory.

If we consider at least the possibility that from the Pentecost of Acts 2 to the *Parousia* at the end of time, those who lost their lives in carrying out their mission are the winners, in what sense are they "reigning"? Are they even now after their deaths "living," or are they extinct? John said that they simultaneously both "came to life and reigned with Christ" (Revelation 20:4). If someone dropped a bomb on every gathered church next Lord's Day, it would just blow us to Heaven. The victories experienced on earth would continue to be enjoyed in Christ's presence. It is time to search the Scriptures for prophetic and apostolic insight into the early church's concepts about the King and His kingdom.

Has the Lord Been Crowned?

A very important theological question must be asked. Can we speak today of Jesus' being King of kings and Lord of lords, or must such terminology be reserved until after the second coming? Has the Lord been crowned? Does He now have "all authority in heaven and on earth" (Matthew 28:18)? Is the kingdom a present reality or only a future hope? Is the evangelistic effort of the church on earth the extension of the Messiah's reign as He rules from His throne in Heaven or only its forerunner?

The book of Revelation has a great deal to say on the topic, for in its pages, in almost every chapter, we see Christ enthroned. Chapters 4 and 5 use the word "throne" seventeen of the forty-seven times it occurs in the book (4:2, 3, 4, 5, 6, 9, 10; 5:1, 6, 7, 11, 13). Always, Christ's throne is in Heaven, although His reign extends over all the earth (Revelation 11:15). Throughout the book, Jesus is "ruler" (1:5), "king" (15:3; 19:16) and "Lord" (19:16). He "reigns" (11:15, 17; 19:16), has "glory" (1:6), "power" (1:6; 12:10), and the "kingdom" (11:15; 12:10).

Can other parts of the Scripture help us in our understanding of this portion of the Holy Bible? I believe so. Look with me, just now, at four passages in the reverse chronological order of their writing. In A.D. 96, the kingdom was a present reality, according to John's Revelation. He spoke both of the book's source as Jesus Christ "the ruler of the kings of the earth" (Revelation 1:5) and the book's recipients as ones made "to be a kingdom" (Revelation 1:6). He began his purpose statement: "I, John, [am] your brother and companion in the ... kingdom" (Revelation 1:9). The apostle believed God's kingdom to be a reality on earth in the days of Domitian. How was it earlier in the time of Vespatian, or just prior to the fall of Jerusalem under Titus in A.D. 70? The author of Hebrews, anticipating that fall, assured the Christians from among the Jewish nation that they had received "a kingdom that cannot be shaken" (Hebrews 12:28). Babylon, Assyria, Persia, Greece, Israel, and even Rome would fall, but not the church. In A.D. 61, Paul reminded the converts in Colossae that they had been "rescued" from Satan's power, or realm, and had been "brought . . . into the kingdom of the Son he loves" (Colossians 1:13). He had written to the Romans some five years before, describing life in that "kingdom of God" as having to do with "righteousness, peace and joy in the Holy Spirit" (Romans 14:17). Whoever has the Spirit of God indwelling his life, and knows the peace and joy flowing from being made righteous by God's grace, has evidence that Christ is reigning in his heart.

Epistles from A.D. 96 (Revelation), 68 (Hebrews), 61 (Colossians), and 56 (Romans) suggest that the kingdom is now here as well as continuing into the hereafter. The words of John the Baptist, Jesus, the Twelve, and the seventy in the years 26 to 30 spoke of the kingdom as coming, and coming soon. The Baptist cried "Repent, for the kingdom of heaven is near" (Matthew 3:2).

Near could either mean "close in time" or "close in space." But Jesus clarified His meaning of *near* to be "close in time" when He said, "I tell you the truth, some who are standing here will not taste death before they see the kingdom of God come with power" (Mark 9:1). The Scripture is clear as to when "the power" came. The disciples, after seeing their Christ alive following His death and burial, were instructed to "stay in the city until you have been clothed with power from on high" (Luke 24:49). That power, they were told, would be theirs "when the Holy Spirit comes on you" (Acts 1:8). On Pentecost Sunday, A.D. 30, the Spirit was given as the first act of Christ's reign at the right hand of the Father. Such was Peter's inspired interpretation on that great day. Jesus was to sit on the Father's right hand until all His enemies were the footstool for His feet. The apostolic declaration was that Jesus was "Lord and Christ" (Acts 2:33-36). We recall the Bible teaching that "the last enemy to be destroyed is death" and that by the resurrection (1 Corinthians 15:26); we are not to look for the kingdom to commense at our resurrection but to be a climactic evidence of that reign.

What a fitting day Pentecost was for the kingdom to begin! That festival had been the memorial of an earlier time when, fifty days after the "passover" at the Exodus, the Ten Commandments had been given and Israel had been constituted God's theocracy. Now, in fulfillment of the type, fifty days after Christ's sacrifice as God's passover lamb, the New Israel would be inaugurated by the giving of the Holy Spirit to indwell Christ's subjects.

Hebrews 1:3 reviews the historic facts, saying, "After he had provided purification for sins, he sat down at the right hand of the Majesty in heaven." Revelation holds the same theology, that at the very time of the writing, Christ already "holds the key of David" (Revelation 3:7). It is safe to say that, prior to the events recorded in Acts 2, the kingdom is spoken of as yet to come; but, after that day, it is spoken of as a present reality (having, nevertheless, a future, eternal dimension; see 2 Peter 1:11; Matthew 25:34).

A text from Daniel is often pointed to as a passage tying the kingdom's inauguration to the return of Jesus. A careful rereading of Daniel 7:13, 14 will make clear that it is when the "one like a son of man" comes "with the clouds of heaven" *to* the Ancient of Days that He is given the kingdom. The preposition is *to,* not *from.* The kingdom is promised at the ascension and not the return of Christ. So did Cyprian (*Testimonies* 2:26) understand the passage, as does today's Church of England, which down through the years has used this text as the lesson on Ascension Day.

Just as the apostles who walked with Jesus reflect His teaching on when His kingdom would come, so they clarify His insight as to its nature. The Old Testament prophecies need to be filtered through the mind of Christ. He understood the prophets in an opposite way from the religious leaders of His place and time. (See 2 Baruch 29:5, 6.) They read Daniel and Isaiah and envisioned an earthly reign: materialistic, Judaistic, and utopian. Gladly would they have followed Jesus as their king, if only He had understood the kingdom prophecies as they did (John 6:15). Jesus, from the beginning of His ministry in the wilderness, had resisted the temptation to rule the world Satan's way (Matthew 4:8-10). We need to take care, at this point, lest the "millennium" we envision become more after the mind of the Pharisees than the thought of the lowly Galilean.

Jesus explained to Pilate, "My kingdom is not of this world. If it were, my servants would fight" (John 18:36). He clarified to the Pharisees, "The kingdom of God does not come with your careful observation, nor will people say, 'Here it is,' or 'There it is,' because the kingdom of God is within you" (Luke 17:20, 21). His followers believed their "citizenship" to be in Heaven (Philippians 3:20) and their weapons to be of a spiritual sort. Paul wrote, "We do not wage war as the world does. The weapons we fight with are not the weapons of the world. On the contrary, they have divine power to demolish strongholds. We demolish arguments and every pretension that sets itself up against the knowledge of God, and we take captive every thought to make it obedient to Christ" (2 Corinthians 10:3-5).

Sin was defeated at Christ's cross. Death was brought to naught at Jesus' resurrection. Having won the victory, He ascended to God's right hand, where He sat down to reign. Under His orders, the church marches across the globe establishing His banner in every clime. During the long duration of the church's advance ("a thousand years"), Satan is powerless to keep the message from being heard. The "gates of Hades will not overcome" (Matthew 16:18). As Daniel foretold, after the world empires of Babylon, Medo-Persia, and Greece, and during the reign of the Romans, "the God of heaven [would] set up a kingdom that will never be destroyed . . . but . . . endure forever" (Daniel 2:44).

To the apostles of Christ, the Old Testament prophecies were about the church, the spiritual descendants of Abraham, Isaac, and Jacob (Acts 15:15-18). To believe as the patriarchs believed was of greater significance than to claim physical ties with them (2 Corinthians 5:16; Galatians 3:6, 7, 26-29). There is one body (Ephesians 4:4) now, not two. The division between Jew and Gentile is gone (Ephesians 2:14, 15). The Church is God's "Israel" (Galatians 6:16; James 1:1; 1 Peter 1:1), God's "circumcision" (Philippians 3:3), for "a man is not a Jew if he is only one outwardly" (Romans 2:28). The apostle to the Gentiles could assure the non-Jewish, newly-baptized converts of his first Gentile mission, "If you belong to Christ, then you are Abraham's seed, and heirs according to the promise" (Galatians 3:29). The Old Testament is to be interpreted by the New Testament, not vice versa. A restoration of Jews to Palestine is unknown in the Christian Scriptures, but their individual salvation is hoped for on the same basis as that of the Gentiles. Romans 11:26 says "so" (οὕτως), or "in the same manner" of believing (John 8:21, 24), would salvation become theirs as the others'. Romans 11:26 is not suggesting that after the first coming, Gentiles will be saved by faith; but, then (τοτέ), after the second coming, the Jews will be saved by sight. The passage teaches that after the first coming and before the second coming, Gentiles will be saved by faith; and during that same time and in exactly that same manner (οὕτως), Jews will be saved.

An earthly rule of a thousand years after Jesus' return would have a difficult time finding a place to exist, for the "earth ... will be burned up" (2 Peter 3:10-13, footnote). It would be in a strait to find a time period in which to fit, for when Jesus returns, it will be at the "last trumpet" (1 Corinthians 15:52), when "the end" arrives and He "hands over the kingdom" (1 Corinthians 15:24) rather than sets it up. When Christ does return, at the final day, it will be to raise the dead (1 Thessalonians 4:15-17), to judge the world (Matthew 25:31, 41), and to bring history to a close (2 Peter 3:10-13). The *parousia* of the Lord will be the end of time and the beginning of eternity.

We are left with a further question relating to Revelation 20. If the church is the kingdom, and the reign of Christ is going on in the gospel age, how are we said to be reigning with Him? Strange as it may seem, similar thoughts run throughout the epistles of the New Testament to describe the present reality—being enjoyed by both writers and readers. The Ephesian church heard the apostolic teaching that God already had made them "alive with Christ." Already, they were "raised ... up with Christ." Already, they were "seated ... with him in the heavenly realms in Christ Jesus" (Ephesians 2:5, 6). This is no different from "the four living creatures and the twenty-four elders" as they found joy in the fact that Jesus had made His blood-purchased flock into "a kingdom ... and they will reign on the earth" (Revelation 5:8-10).

The church in every community is an outpost of the kingdom of Heaven. The King of England, in earlier times, ruled over his Commonwealth without being physically present in every part of it. It is often pointed out that the throne of Christ is in Heaven and not on earth (Revelation 1:4; 4:2-6, 9, 10; 5:6, 7, 11, 13; 6:16; 7:9-11, 15, 17; 8:3; 12:5; 14:3; 16:17; 19:4; 21:5; 22:1, 3) and that after death he that overcomes will sit down on Christ's throne, as He overcame and sat down on His Father's throne (Revelation 3:21). There is no question that "the souls of those who had been beheaded because of their testimony for Jesus" (Revelation 20:4) share in the victories Christ continues to accomplish from His Heavenly throne. But this does not lessen the other side of the truth that before death, while in His service here, we in a sense are reigning already.

In what sense are we reigning now? We know how it is with the apostles, Christ's "ambassadors" (2 Corinthians 5:10). "At the renewal of all things, when the Son of Man sits on his glorious throne," said Jesus to His apostles, "you ... will also sit on twelve thrones, judging the twelve tribes of Israel" (Matthew 19:28). The time of "renewal" or new birth (that is, the gospel age when men can find new life in Christ) is to find the Twelve sharing in the reign. They are lawmakers for the King. "Whatever [they] bind on earth will be bound in heaven" (Matthew 16:19). Christ is the ultimate authority in the kingdom; but He has delegated to His apostles the power of revealing His orders. That being the case, the church follows the faith and practice of "the apostles' teaching" (Acts 2:42). Their ministry was to the church universal, the church of all times and all localities. That teaching, now written in the New Testament documents, serves as the norm for Christianity in every age.

Consider how elders of local congregations share in Christ's rule. As every synagogue in Jesus' day was under the care of the rulers of that synagogue, every congregation in our day is under the shepherding care of elders. The believers were instructed, "Obey your leaders and submit to their authority. They keep watch over you as men who must give an account" (Hebrews 13:17). Elders had no power to legislate or to make rules, but were authorized to see that Christ's rules from His apostles were carried out in their sphere of authority, a local church. That was their share in reigning or ruling with Christ.

Every teacher of a Bible class and every parent entrusted with a child to nurture can extend Christ's reign. He or she extends Christ's rule by holding forth Jesus' teaching in word and example, stating and enforcing it, living and propagating it. This can be done now as well as in the future. If Jeremiah, by the words of God in his mouth, could rule over nations, both overthrowing and building (Jeremiah 1:9, 10), God's workers today share the victories of conquest as well as in the tribulations of the battle.

John, even though banished to the isle of Patmos, knew of victories already gained. He who considered Jesus as reigning ("glorified") from a cross (John 12:23-25, 13:31) would not but see himself sharing in "the suffering and kingdom" (Revelation 1:9) at one and the same time.

Did a Trumpet Sound?

Whatever the millennium is, or however the souls reign, that time and rule is preceded and followed by a "resurrection," according to Revelation 20:4, 5. Some Bible teachers insist that if one of these resurrections is physical, so must the other be; or, if one is spiritual, a similar meaning must be given to the other.

That requirement sounds strange to me in the light of John's authorship of both the Gospel of John and the Revelation. In the Gospel, John recorded Jesus' teaching about two births. Nicodemus, you remember, was told by Jesus that the natural birth was not enough. He "must be born again [anew]" (John 3:7). Physical birth, without the spiritual birth of "water and the Spirit" (John 3:5), would fail to bring a man into "the kingdom of God."

Even more appropriate, as the interpretive key of Revelation 20, is the passage of John 5, where two resurrections were the topic of Jesus' discussion with His critics. One of the resurrections was of a spiritual nature and was going on in the present day. The other was a physical resurrection to take place at the end of history. Recall the Lord's words regarding the two types and times of resurrection. Regarding the present, He said, "I tell you the truth, a time is coming and has now come when the dead will hear the voice of the Son of God and those who hear will live" (John 5:25). Regarding the general resurrection of bodies at the end of time, He taught, "A time is coming when all who are in their graves will hear his voice and come out—those who have done good will rise to live, and those who have done evil will rise to be condemned" (John 5:28).

What have we learned? If you are born once, you will die twice; but if you are born twice, you will die only once. If you are born of your earthly mother by physical birth into the physical world, but are never born from above of the Heavenly Father (that is, converted to Christ), you will experience more than the physical death that befalls all mortals. Those not born again, or born the second time, will undergo what Revelation calls "the second death" (Revelation 20:14). But, if in addition to the physical birth, there is the spiritual birth of which Christ speaks, then you will die but once. As all men since Adam, Christ's followers will die, but they will not face the second death, the eternal separation from God.

Behind the opinion that conversion to the Lord Jesus is the essential "first resurrection" stand other texts from Christ and His apostles. "Blessed and holy are those who have part in the first resurrection. The second death has no power over them," wrote John (Revelation 20:6). How did his Master and his colleagues think on this theme?

Not every "resurrection" of Scripture is a reference to the physical resurrection at time's end. Ezekiel's vision of dry bones coming together and being enfleshed was a symbol for the Jews' return to the land of Palestine after their Babylonian captivity (Ezekiel 37:1-14). More importantly, to Christ, when prodigals return to their Father, that is a resurrection indeed. In the beautiful parable of the Prodigal Son, the Father's words to his other son about the younger boy who had returned home were, "We had to celebrate and be glad, because this brother of yours was dead and is alive again; he was lost and is found" (Luke 15:32).

How often, at the baptism of a new convert, the words of Paul are read: "Don't you know that all of us who were baptized into Christ Jesus were baptized into his death? We were therefore buried with him through baptism into death in order that, just as Christ was raised from the dead through the glory of the Father, we too may live a new life. If we have been united with him like this in his death, we will certainly also be united with him in his resurrection" (Romans 6:3-5). Conversion is a resurrection! "Having been buried with him in baptism and raised with him [Christ] through your faith in the power of God" (Colossians 2:12), the immersed believer can be exhorted, "Since, then, you have been raised with Christ, set your hearts on things above, where Christ is seated at the right hand of God. Set your minds on things above.... For you died, and your life is now hidden with Christ in God" (Colossians 3:1-3).

To think as these early followers of Christ thought is to recognize that, before conversion, people "were dead in ... transgressions and sins" (Ephesians 2:1). By grace, God quickened them. In the apostle's words, God "made us alive with Christ even when we were dead.... And God raised us up with Christ and seated us with him in the heavenly realms" (Ephesians 2:5, 6). Colossian Christians, Ephesian Christians, Roman Christians, and American Christians, as their brothers and sisters everywhere, have undergone the blessed first resurrection of conversion from death to life.

If the resurrection that leads to Satan's binding for the thousand years may be the spiritual resurrection of conversion that saves from the "second death," what is the other resurrection that concludes the millennium of time? Jesus' similar teaching in John 5 may surprise you. He seems to envision the physical resurrection from the "graves" of two classes—good and evil. But He appears not to be thinking of two times a thousand years apart. Instead, He envisions one time called "a time [that] is coming" (John 5:28, 29). Such a general resurrection of "all who are in their graves" at Christ's return is implied in Revelation 1:7, where those beholding Jesus' return "with the clouds" will include "those who pierced him." To believe this necessitates the resurrection at Christ's coming to include the wicked as well as the righteous—the pagan Roman soldiers who put the nails in His hands and the spear in His side as well as Mary and John.

"A resurrection of both the righteous and the wicked" are Paul's words to describe an event that will include two groups (Acts 24:15). "Some to everlasting life, others to shame and everlasting contempt" are Daniel's words about the consequence accompanying the "multitudes who sleep in the dust of the earth" as they are awakened to judgment (Daniel 12:2).

You ask when the dead shall rise? Aside from Revelation 20, the Bible's answer is at the conclusion of all human history. Jesus encouraged His followers with the teaching: "And this is the will of him who sent me, that I shall lose none of all that he has given me, but raise them up at the last day. For my Father's will is that everyone that looks to the Son and believes in him shall have eternal life, and I will raise him up at the last day" (John 6:39, 40). Martha's understanding was that Lazarus would "rise again in the resurrection at the last day" (John 11:24). Paul received no different information, timing his resurrection "at the last trumpet" (1 Corinthians 15:52), rather than some thousand years before the "last" day or its "last" trumpet.

With the words and phrases from the rest of the New Testament ringing in our ears, as we read the first verses of Revelation 20, we see the first resurrection as the conversion of the soul and the second as the resurrection of the body. "The souls of those who had been beheaded because of their testimony for Jesus and because of the word of God ... [who had] not worshiped the beast" (Revelation 20:4) represent all who "have been crucified with Christ" (Galatians 2:20). Is not every person who has died to sin "holy" and "blessed"? Do not all believers become "priests of God" and escape "the second death" (Revelation 20:6)?

What remains is to place the binding of Satan into such a scheme of thought. If the book of Revelation, including its millennium, is to be taken symbolically, a key has been found. If Jesus now reigns from the Heavenly Jerusalem and needs await no coronation in the earthly one, the King has been crowned. If the gospel trumpeted calls men from death to life, and those trusting in the risen Christ are resurrected from watery graves to walk in newness of life, then already it can be said a trumpet did sound. In the world where the "devil prowls around like a roaring lion looking for someone to devour" (1 Peter 5:8), can it be claimed the devil has been bound?

Has the Devil Been Bound?

The "destruction" of Satan is not the question. It is the "binding" of man's enemy that we consider. The act of God toward the deceiver is, in the early verses of our chapter, preventative. At the end of the chapter, it will be punitive. He who is first "bound" (Revelation 20:1, 2) will, in the end, be "thrown into the lake of burning sulfur.... [and] will be tormented day and night for ever and ever" (Revelation 20:10). When Peter and Paul were in "chains" (Acts 12:6; 2 Timothy 1:16), they still had great influence for their cause. Satan's limited influence is still to be dealt with.

We see the picture, as John painted it, of "an angel coming down out of heaven, having the key to the Abyss and holding in his hand a great chain" (Revelation 20:1). We understand that Satan is a spirit-being that no literal chain could restrain. But we know God is behind the limitation to come upon the devil, for His servant who will do the binding comes "down out of heaven." The church needs both literal and symbolic reminders that their opponent is not almighty. God's family needs to remember that Satan is alive, lest they become too optimistic in this world. They need also to remember he is limited in what he can do even now, lest they become too pessimistic or discouraged.

If the gangster of recent memory, Al Capone, could be said to rule Chicago's underworld even from his jail cell, we should be able to grasp that Satan, even with the divine restrictions put upon him, is to be recognized. But, restricted he is! "No temptation has seized you except what is common to man. And God is faithful; he will not let you be tempted beyond what you can bear. But when you are tempted, he will also provide a way out so that you can stand up under it" (1 Corinthians 10:13). Satan is limited in power.

He who has all power and "all authority in heaven and on earth" has ordered the nations evangelized (Matthew 28:18-20). When He earlier commissioned the seventy[16] to preach in Perea, they "returned with joy and said, 'Lord, even the demons submit to us in your name.'" Jesus responded, "I saw Satan fall like lightning from heaven" (Luke 10:17, 18). Paul lifted the spirits of the Roman congregation with the words, "The God of peace will soon crush Satan under your feet" (Romans 16:20). Jesus, by parable, predicted the kingdom would grow like a "mustard seed" from the tiny to the tremendous (Matthew 13:31, 32) and it would work like yeast affecting all that into which it was placed (Matthew 13:33). The "gates," or defenses, of Satan's domain will not "overcome" the church on the march (Matthew 16:18).

The concept of the binding of Satan is not new to Revelation. Sixty years earlier, Jesus explained that His ability to enter Satan's realm and free the demon-possessed was evidence of His power, surpassing that of the devil. He said, "How can anyone enter a strong man's house and carry off his possessions unless he first ties up the strong man? Then he can rob his house" (Matthew 12:29).

Learn that Jesus' ministry was a binding of Satan. Learn that Jesus' death was a despoiling of "the powers and authorities" (Colossians 2:15). Learn that on the cross there was the destruction of "him who holds the power of death—that is, the devil" (Hebrews 2:14). Learn that in Christ's passion "the prince of this world will be driven [thrown] out" (John 12:31). How similar is

---

[16] Or "seventy-two." See Luke 10:1, including the footnote, in NIV.

this last terminology to John's later words, that the angel "threw [the old serpent being] into the abyss" (Revelation 20:3) and Peter's words about the fallen angels, that God "sent them [threw them down] to hell (τάρταρος), putting them into gloomy dungeons" (2 Peter 2:4).

If Satan's being cast down is in the will of God, his loosing "for a short time" is also by the permission of the Almighty. Satan cannot break his own chains. To approach a house where two guard dogs are chained in the front yard calls for sufficient wisdom to judge accurately the length of the chains. Wherein has God limited Satan in this age? He has not permitted him "to deceive the nations" (Revelation 20:8) into suppressing successfully Christ's church as it spreads the story of the cross from Jerusalem "to the ends of the earth" (Acts 1:8). Let the church be busy at its task, while the door is opened, for missionary opportunities will not last forever. Just before the end of the age, all Hell breaks loose in a final effort to marshall every anti-Christian force against the message. So harsh will be the defeated foe's final effort that the question can be posed, "When the Son of Man comes, will he find faith on the earth?" (Luke 18:8). Yet, after a short while, Christ will be back to destroy the enemy and time will be replaced by eternity. Until that glorious day, let the church push the advance of the Gospel.

The Perspective of Endurance

CHAPTER FOUR

The Perspective of Endurance
"Your . . . Companion in the . . . Patient Endurance"

It is profitable to read Revelation from the perspective of endurance. The book's symbols alert us to expect tribulation from the world to which we bring God's message. But they also encourage us to anticipate success across that world as the kingdom is extended to all peoples. Opposition and advance, suffering and reigning, are but two sides of the same coin. The tribulation is the result of being in the kingdom. If we were not carrying out the orders of Christ, the opposition of the world would not be directed against us. Since God's intense love for His creatures could not be discouraged by rejection, Jesus endured the cross rather than turn from His effort to save the lost. So His church has not in the past, and must not in the future, be turned aside from its divine directive to bring the good news "to all creation" (Mark 16:15). This calls for the Christlike quality of steadfastness.

Steadfastness and *patient endurance* are English equivalents of the Greek word ὑπομονή. Ὑπο means "under." The other half of the Greek word means "to remain." Literally, then, John's term calls for all the readers "to remain under" the load placed upon their shoulders. No follower of the Crucified One should step out from under the burden of responsibility to share with others the story that has so blessed his or her own life. Souls are being parched by the searing rays of condemnation. Should hardship turn us aside from bringing the refreshing water of life to men in agony? Others suffered to get help to us. We dare not let tribulation divert us from the mission of mercy. However we understand the "millennium" or other topics relating to prophecy and the end of the age, stick-to-itiveness that never lets go should mark every Christian as he brings the Savior to his lost world.

The book of Revelation is intended to produce hope, to instill courage, and to call for loyalty and faithful endurance. Let the reader beware of growing weary (Revelation 2:3) or forsaking his first love (2:4). Let him avoid denying either his faith (2:13) or Christ's name (3:8). Let him watch out for the danger of becoming lukewarm or useless (3:16). Rather than faltering, let the reader overcome (2:7, 11, 17; 3:5, 12, 21). Let him hold on (2:25) and remain true (2:13). Let him be earnest (3:19), keeping what is written (1:3; 2:26; 3:8; 22:9) and doing what is commanded. Being "true" is a description of Jesus (3:14; 19:11) and His words (22:6). It ought to be said of His followers that they, too, are faithful (2:10).

It helps workers in the struggle to remember that John did not give this counsel of patience from the easy-chair of some comfortable office. He was their "brother and companion in the suffering" (Revelation 1:9). He, from Patmos, could have written a new record of more recent sufferers-for-the-faith than had been listed earlier in the book of Hebrews (chapter 11). Had he done so, he likely would have made a similar concluding appeal: "Therefore, since we are surrounded by such a great a cloud of witnesses, let us throw off everything that hinders and the sin that so easily entangles, and let us run with perseverance the race marked out for us. Let us fix our eyes on Jesus, the author and perfecter of our faith, who for the joy set before him endured the cross, scorning its shame, and sat down at the right hand of the throne of God. Consider him who endured such opposition from sinful men, so that you will not grow weary and lose heart" (Hebrews 12:1-3).

Tribulation and patient endurance are inseparable companions. Paul called on his contemporaries to "rejoice in our sufferings, because we know that suffering produces perseverance" (Romans 5:3). James urged his dispersed Jerusalem congregation, "Consider it pure joy . . . whenever you face trials of many kinds, because you know that the testing of your faith develops perseverance" (James 1:2, 3). He concluded his letter reminding the brethren that "we consider blessed those who have persevered" and encouraging the church to remember "Job's perseverance" (James 5:11).

It may be more exciting to hear a prophetic lecture that pinpoints by names and dates the events to precede Christ's return than to discuss suffering and perseverance. But the latter is more essential. Our future demands that we heed the Spirit's call for loyalty to the evangelistic task until Jesus' return.

Throughout the book of Revelation, there rings the cry, "He who has an ear, let him hear what the Spirit says to the churches" (Revelation 2:7). This line was repeated to every congregation addressed (2:11, 17, 29; 3:6, 13, 22), plus one additional time for good measure (13:9). The Spirit of God was speaking—*is* speaking. He was speaking to the churches. He was speaking on a theme essential to their survival. But they were not listening.

Are we listening? The words were not meant for just Ephesus or Thyatira. They come to "churches." Note the plural. The warnings are for congregations in all times and places.

It is frightening to remember that those who first received the Revelation thought they were listening but were not. The record is that, of the seven churches addressed in chapters 1, 2, and 3, six out of seven had the candlestick removed. Visit the area today and see mosques where once the church thrived, and abruptly you are made aware that past evangelistic triumphs dare not lull us to complacency. The "first love" of sharing one's faith must not be lost. Even an Ephesian church that enjoyed personal ministries by Paul and John can be removed as a light-bearing entity when the Spirit's plea to repent goes unheeded. I have no doubt that you would have met a strong argument from all those existent churches had you implied that they were not in good spiritual shape or that they were losing thrust in carrying out their mission. Yet, the sad history is that the churches with such great pasts did not overcome in the present and lost the future. Smyrna, with all its persecution, survived by being "faithful, even to the point of death" (Revelation 2:10).

To "overcome," or to have "victory" (νικάω), is God's will for His church. John loved that word and used it twenty-four of the twenty-seven times it appears in the New Testament. He wrote the word once in his Gospel, six times in his first epistle, but seventeen times in his Revelation. While the word in extra-Biblical writings speaks of something *taken* by the powerful of the world, in the New Testament, it refers to what is *given* by Christ to those who are faithful to Him. Our human resources are fatally inadequate, but His divine resource will give victory if we are but faithful. He will speak, "Well done, good and faithful servant!" (Matthew 25:21). He looks not for success, but for fortitude and faithfulness. To such, He guarantees victory.

To wear the mark of the best (the Christ) and not the mark of the beast (the antichrist) ought to be the believer's desire. The former is described in the last verses of chapter 16 and the latter in the first verses of chapter 17. To avoid the catastrophe of wearing the stamp of doom and to be assured of the joy in bearing the seal of the saved, three things are demanded. We must rely on the Savior's vow, recognize the serpent's voice, and receive the saint's victory.

Rely on the Savior's Vow

When Jesus gives to you a promise, or makes to you a vow, you can depend on it. We speak of baptismal vows. We share in marital vows. Soldiers make military vows. In any covenant situation, there are parties, terms, and promises. The church lives under what the Scriptures call the "new covenant" (Hebrews 8:8). The church can rely upon the promises Christ has made to us. Can He depend upon the promise we made to Him at the time of our conversion when we accepted Him as Savior and Lord? Prior to rehearing what He expects of those in covenant with Him, be reminded of His covenantal words to you.

When it comes to faithfulness to agreements, one need never worry about Jesus' breaking a promise. Listen to Paul: "If we are faithless, he will remain faithful, for he cannot disown himself" (2 Timothy 2:13). Hear the author of Hebrews quote the Old Testament lines, "Never will I leave you; never will I forsake you" (Hebrews 13:5). Sing the hymn based on James 1:17:

> "Great is Thy faithfulness, O God my Father
> There is no shadow of turning with Thee;
> Thou changest not, Thy compassions they fail not;
> As Thou hast been, Thou forever wilt be." [17]

The book of Revelation reveals a Savior who vows to support His Word, shepherd His flock, and subdue His enemies. You can count on it. As Messiah, or Anointed One, He is God's Prophet, Priest, and King. As Prophet, He vows to support His Word. As Priest, He pledges to pastor and shepherd His flock all the way

---

[17] "Great Is Thy Faithfulness" by Thomas O. Chisholm. Copyright 1923. Renewal 1951 by W. M. Runyon. Assigned to Hope Publishing Company. All rights reserved. Used by permission.

to glory. As King, He assures that He will subdue all enemies. Our commitments to Him are the easier to sustain in loyalty by the awareness that His words to us will never be broken.

The Vow to Support His Word

The Revelation that came to John on Patmos came from the "witness" Jesus Christ (Revelation 1:5). One adjective precedes the word *witness*. It is the vital word *faithful*. Jesus is no false witness or uninformed witness; He is a "faithful witness." Did these scenes, passing before the prophetic eyes, seem too good to be true? John had no hesitancy about recording what he saw and heard, nor let any reader have any doubts about accepting what he reads, "for these words are trustworthy and true" (Revelation 21:5).

The words of men often fail us, for men sometimes lie intentionally. In other cases, their words cannot be counted on because, in spite of the best of intentions, they become unable to do what they promised. Perhaps you recall loaning money to a friend who assured you of repayment by the next Friday, when he would get his paycheck, only to learn that the computer broke down and the check would be delayed. God, however, who knows the end from the beginning, commits himself to us and proves to be the faithful and true witness in every instance. God is a God of His word. In the phraseology of Hebrews 6:18, "It is impossible for God to lie." Lying is not within His nature who is the Truth. What He reveals in His Word, you can count on. Jesus put His stamp of approval on the entire Old Testament when He said, "The Scripture cannot be broken" (John 10:35). The word of mortal man is frail and breakable. Not so with the word of Almighty God. Jesus' own teaching was often preceded by the words, "Amen, amen, I say unto you," or as the King James says, "Verily, verily. . . ." The NIV generally renders it, "I tell you the truth." However we translate it, the phrase calls attention to the dependability of that which the Lord will speak. What Jesus uttered from Matthew to Revelation is just as reliable as Solomon found of God's words through Moses: "Not one word has failed of all the good promises he gave" (1 Kings 8:56).

Each of the seven letters in Revelation 2 and 3 concludes with a promise from the Christ, who supports His word. The seven letters follow a structure. After an introduction, which matches

Jesus' abilities as described in the vision of chapter 1 with the particular needs of a certain congregation, there follows what is right with that church, what is wrong with that church, what is needed by that church, and then (for motivation) what is promised to that church. This promise is meant to assure the believers that they can straighten up and all will go well. In nearly every case, Jesus looked for something to commend so He could point out their good points. Loving them, He next turned to their bad points that called for correction. After isolating their needs, He gave a word of promise.

Every individual, like every congregation, having pledged allegiance earlier, ought to respond to the dependable promises of Christ in faithfulness. In doing so, there will be blessings untold (Revelation 2:7, 11, 17, 26-28; 3:5, 12, 21). As Paul prayed decades before, John would plead to the Father for his converts: "May the Lord direct your hearts into God's love and Christ's perseverance" (2 Thessalonians 3:5).

The Vow to Shepherd His Flock

God's only begotten Son will never fail or forsake His people (Hebrews 13:5). They can be assured that His Word is reliable. He vows to support His Word and to shepherd His people. His flock, His New Israel, He will guide from their Egyptian bondage of sin, across the deserts of adversity, and into their promised land of glory.

Note the mixture of figures in Revelation. It is the "Lamb" that "will be their shepherd; he will lead them to springs of living water" (Revelation 7:17). The Lamb, offered in sacrifice for the world's sins, is the kind Shepherd who leads those He has purchased all the way to His eternal home. The author of Hebrews tied the sacrifice of Calvary to the shepherding of the Crucified One when he referred to Jesus as "that great Shepherd of the sheep" in the same breath as he mentioned "the blood of the eternal covenant" (Hebrews 13:20).

He who is true to His Word is true to His people. He who keeps His promises keeps His sheep. No Christian can read the twenty-third Psalm without mentally seeing Jesus as the shepherd described. David wrote, "The Lord is my shepherd; I shall lack nothing" (Psalm 23:1). After writing about "green pastures" and "quiet waters," he affirmed, "Surely goodness and love will follow me all the days of my life." No period is placed there. He put an *and,* for there is something more, a great deal more. He continued, "And I will dwell in the house of the Lord forever" (Psalm 23:6). Not in this world alone does the believer have wonderful guidance. He has it hereafter.

Let every present-day pastor remember his model in Christ. A pastoral painting is that scene where a shepherd is on the hillside with his sheep. "Pastor" and "pasture" go together, for the pastor is in the pasture tending and guiding and feeding his flock. Christ has placed under-shepherds in His church as gifts for the blessing of His flock. "He ... gave some ... to be pastors" (Ephesians 4:11). Such elders (Acts 20:17) were admonished with the words, "Keep watch over yourselves and all the flock of which the Holy Spirit has made you overseers. Be shepherds of the church of God, which he bought with his own blood" (Acts 20:28).

John's imagery of Christ as shepherd in Revelation should be viewed in light of the similar imagery in his Gospel. John 10 contrasts "the good shepherd" of the sheep with undependable "hired hands." Hired hands run when trouble comes (John 10:12, 13). They lack the quality of steadfastness and patience that God sees in His Son and seeks in His followers. When "wolves" or "dragons" threaten, let each believer remember how reliable is our example. He said, "My sheep listen to my voice; I know them, and they follow me. I give them eternal life, and they shall never perish; no one can snatch them out of my hand" (John 10:27, 28).

The Vow to Subdue His Enemies

I am helped to remain loyal to Jesus by remembering His complete reliability. As God's anointed Prophet, He shows himself true to His Word. As the Heavenly Father's anointed Priest, He proves true to His people, guiding them as a gentle shepherd. His rod of iron, or "iron scepter" (Revelation 2:27; 12:5; 19:15), ought to be feared by attacking enemies, while His kindly shepherding ought to be followed by appreciative sheep. As Heaven's anointed King, He is pictured as true to His mission. All enemies shall become the footstool for His feet (Acts 2:35).

The world is ever filled with kings that "will make war against the Lamb." But rest assured, "the Lamb will overcome them because he is Lord of lords and King of kings—and with him will be his called, chosen and faithful followers" (Revelation 17:14).

In Daniel, the beasts represented the world empires with which Israel had to deal. In Revelation, the beasts likewise picture the various types of opposition that Christ's New Israel must face. Snarling and fiercesome as they may be, or strong and deceptive as their powers may seem, they are no match for the One who sits on David's throne. In the end, as the seventh angel sounds, the verdict of Heavenly hosts is that "the kingdom of the world has become the kingdom of our Lord and of his Christ, and he will reign for ever and ever" (Revelation 11:15).

John's carefully designed mural of world history pictures the rise and fall of God's enemies. Chapters 12-17 describe the rise, and chapters 18-20, the fall. Careful note should be given to the fact that the demise of the opponents of Heaven is in approximately the reverse order to their origin. We meet first the dragon himself in Revelation 12. He is "an enormous red dragon with seven heads and ten horns" (12:3), "that ancient serpent called the devil or Satan, who leads the whole world astray" (12:9). His cohorts are the two dreadful beasts (one from the sea and one from the earth) described in chapter 13 and a scarlet woman associated with them in chapter 17.

The first to fall is the prostitute. "Babylon," as the prostitute is named (17:5), falls in total ruin in chapter 18. This leads to the hallelujah chorus of chapter 19. The next to collapse are the beast (from the sea) and the "false prophet" (the beast from the earth). Both enemies are condemned to the lake of fire (19:20). The twentieth chapter finds the dragon meeting the same fate (20:10). The eternal joys of the new heaven and earth, painted in bright, livid colors in the final chapters of Revelation, are preceded by the rise and then the defeat of all the hosts of Hell. "Thanks be to God, who always leads us in triumphal procession in Christ" (2 Corinthians 2:14).

Avoid receiving the mark of ownership by a certainly defeated foe. Make every effort to bear the seal of approval by the victor, Christ. The first requisite for this we have labeled reliance on the Savior's vow that He will support His Word, shepherd His sheep, and subdue His opponents. The second essential is the recognition of the serpent's voice.

Recognize the Serpent's Voice

Ever since the garden of Eden, Satan has been a "murderer" (John 8:44). To this hour, we need the apostolic injunction: "Be self-controlled and alert. Your enemy the devil prowls around like a roaring lion looking for someone to devour" (1 Peter 5:8). The devil's stock and trade is deception. His success with men is that he makes error sound like truth and evil appear to be good. John called him the one "who leads the whole world astray" (Revelation 12:9). To protect the Christians from this master of deception, John warned his readers not to accept all they were hearing, even in the assemblies, as the voice of the true shepherd. Let us listen with care for the hiss of the serpent. Let us never think that the devil hands out elixir labeled "Poison." If he did, who would drink it? The sly serpent rather puts but a dash of strychnine in an attractive glass of refreshing brew, assuring that it won't hurt you. He will say to you, as he did to Eve, "You will not surely die. . . . your eyes will be opened, and you will be like God" (Genesis 3:4, 5).

Satan comes in a variety of guises, all of them attractive. Wanting to deceive, he will not come dressed in horns and forked tail, nor holding a pitchfork. He will be garbed in a way that will be appealing to his next victim. You must be on the lookout. He will appear in three forms in three arenas. I understand John's classifications as politics, preaching, and principles. When Satan enters these arenas, we have politics gone awry, preaching off course, and principles totally disowned.

Politics That Is Antichrist

The two beasts that serve the dragon's purposes are introduced in Revelation 13. One comes out of the land and the other rises out of the sea. Satan will work through them both. As God's mission to save the world will be carried out through His church, Satan's plan to destroy that world will be furthered by his own tools.

John lived in an hour when the Roman government that had been "God's servant to do . . . good" (Romans 13:4) had become a destructive force against what was good. Government, *per se*, is good. "Everyone," according to Paul in Romans 13, was to "submit himself to the governing authorities." According to John, in Revelation 13, an earthly power ordained to be a terror to evil and an ally of good can betray that mission. Football or basketball games would be chaos without rules and referees. Only anarchy and riot prevail when every man does what is right in his own eyes, caring nothing for others. Hence, government, in itself, is good. But government, ignoring God and suppressing truth, becomes bestial in nature. A totalitarian state, replacing God and good, becomes inhuman. It uses monstrous power to trample on people as though they were things.

Government, fulfilling its divinely intended function, restrains evil by law and order (2 Thessalonians 2:6). The Rome that Luke reflects in the book of Acts was a friend to the minority and protector of the innocent. That government, like many before and since, became an instrument of oppression. Revelation 13:1-10 describes the beastly character of politics devoid of goodness. Domitian's rule was pagan rule at its worst. The crowns, or diadems, on the ten horns (Revelation 13:1) symbolized that might, rather than right, was reigning at the time. Men were being treated as commodities. Seven heads may stand for Rome's emperors from Augustus to Domitian, omitting the rebellions of Galbus, Otho, and Vitelius, or more likely, for all kings and kingdoms past, present, and future that ally with Satan against God.

Preaching That Is Antichrist

Are you willing to get closer to home? Russia or China or any other state in the Eastern or Western block can be a Satanic tool impeding the church in its mission. But can the driver of a car with the bumper sticker reading "Clergy" ever get off course and advance Satan's cause rather than that of Christ? Does the devil ever use the mouth of a person standing behind the pulpit of a church? Will careful listening to what is said reveal the Shepherd's voice, or might it echo the hiss of the serpent? Especially when religion unites with state, encouraging people to bow down to the beast, there is danger of the voice of man being taken as the voice of God.

The beast that rose "out of the earth" was a religious entity. He caused men to "worship the first beast" and "performed great and miraculous signs" (Revelation 13:12, 13). He appeared to be like a "lamb" but has a voice like "a dragon" (13:11).

Had not Jesus warned His disciples to "watch out for false prophets [who] come to you in sheep's clothing, but inwardly ... are ferocious wolves" (Matthew 7:15)? Can we not add that history observes pseudoteachers coming also in shepherd's clothing? Paul was wise enough to see that even "Satan himself masquerades as an angel of light" (2 Corinthians 11:14). *Angel* means messenger. The light to which Paul referred is the light of the gospel. He observed that our enemy is never more successful in deception than when he carries a Bible or wears a garb that suggests he represents the thoughts of God while he propagates a darkness parading as light. A part of the devilish scheme is to use the very words that true apostles had used and believers had accepted, but to alter their original meanings. To the Galatian church, the warning against Judaizers was raised. Only careful ears would hear "a different gospel—which is really no gospel at all" from teachers who would "pervert" or change the "gospel of Christ" (Galatians 1:6, 7). Every man must be wise as a serpent (Matthew 10:16) not to be misled by the serpent that deceives the world. His tactics are as old as time. Where ancient Scripture contained the message "men spoke from God as they were carried along by the Holy Spirit," the Jewish nation had their share of false prophets that misled Israel. Let the church not be *naive*. "There will be false teachers among you. They will secretly introduce destructive heresies" (2 Peter 1:21—2:2).

Christ found it commendable that the saints at Ephesus could not tolerate wicked men and had tested those who claimed to be apostles, but were not (Revelation 2:2). Luke called it exemplary that Bereans "examined the Scriptures every day to see if what Paul said was true" (Acts 17:11). To accept any teaching being handed out as the gospel truth, without putting it to the test of Scripture, is fatal to God's flock. We are to "test everything" and "hold on to [*only*] the good" (1 Thessalonians 5:21). We are urged, "Do not believe every spirit, but test the spirits to see whether they are from God, because many false prophets have gone out into the world" (1 John 4:1). How can the test be made? Hear Christ's beloved disciple as he speaks for all the inspired writers: "We are from God, and whoever knows God listens to us; but whoever is not from God does not listen to us. This is how we recognize the Spirit of truth and the spirit of falsehood" (1 John 4:6). Thou shalt not accept everything preachers say. Thou shalt check it by Christ's teaching, as passed on to the church through His inspired Word, especially the New Covenant.

Principles That Are Antichrist

Where chapter 13 of Revelation introduced us to two allies of the dragon, chapter 17 showed us another. Pagan governments often threaten the church, as do pagan religions. In area after area, the mission work of Christian forces is driven back by a political entity or a religious group. Satan, on occasion, uses the first beast. At another time, he harnesses the skills of the false prophet. Many a worker for Christ has been under the fire of both beasts combined. When that fails, Satan turns to a third ally, pagan philosophy. In one of its forms, this earthly thinking becomes the "playboy philosophy" so acceptable to modern man. It was painted by John under the imagery of a woman who causes men to fall, as they are "intoxicated with the wine of her adulteries" (Revelation 17:2).

The church of the Lord is "clothed with the sun, with the moon under her feet" (Revelation 12:1). Yet, to the earth-dwellers, there is an attraction for the other woman, "dressed in purple and scarlet, and ... glittering with gold, precious stones and pearls. She held a golden cup in her hand, filled with abominable things and the filth of her adulteries" (Revelation 17:4).

If, in the night, the world's way of thinking seems to have an attraction, turn on the lights and look again. The world may call you "Victorian." They may ridicule you for holding to absolutes when the intellectual institutions turned them out-of-doors long ago. But lest you be destroyed in the chaos this Babylonian thinking creates, hear the angelic voice saying, "Come out of her, my people, so that you will not share in her sins, so that you will not receive any of her plagues" (Revelation 18:4).

Should a creature of God follow the advice, "If it feels good, do it"? Should human acts follow the glands of man's body or the guidance of God's book? The earliest followers of Jesus chose to be slaves (δοῦλοι) of Christ Jesus (Philippians 1:1). A "servant" would have some thoughts and hours he could call his own. But a "slave" only existed to carry out the will of another. Foreign chemicals injected into the body enslave one's mind to the dragon. The lasting lift that sets free is the higher high coming from the Lamb who is Lord.

What a cesspool is the moral atmosphere of the world! What a loathsome sight is the harlot! Satan would dethrone the almighty God and redefine what is good. Even some, in the name of religion, defy Bible definitions of right and wrong or acceptable and unacceptable behavior by redefinition. But He who claimed to have "all authority in heaven and on earth" (Matthew 28:18) left not a smidgen of authority for human governments or man-made churches to outvote Him. Since zero plus zero equals zero, the unanimous vote of the human race on abortion or euthanasia or homosexuality or liberation theology or any other moral issues will not change by a milligram or a centimeter the everlasting standard of God, the norm of good. As the Psalmist sang, "Your word, O Lord, is eternal; it stands firm in the heavens" (Psalm 119:89).

Christ's sheep hear His voice and follow it. "But they will never follow a stranger; in fact, they will run away from him because they do not recognize a stranger's voice" (John 10:5). Woe to those who cannot distinguish between the hiss of a snake and the voice of the Savior.

Receive the Saint's Victory

What is the mark of the beast, Satan's antichrist? What is the mark of the best, God's Messiah? Both those who follow the Lord and those who follow the devil bear a brand. Revelation 13 concludes: "He [the beast] also forced everyone . . . to receive a mark on his right hand or on his forehead . . . the mark, which is the name of the beast or the number of his name. . . . it is man's number. His number is 666" (Revelation 13:16-18). Revelation 14 begins: "Then I looked, and there before me was the Lamb . . . and with him 144,000 who had his name and his Father's name written on their foreheads" (14:1).

Many are the characters on the stage of history that someone has nominated as the beast personified. In some quarters, it is suggested that the Roman Pontif wears a triple tiara with the Latin words *"VICARIVS FILII DEI,"* which, counting the numerical value of the letters that are also Roman numerals, adds up to 666. Many prefer the Hebrew spelling of *Neron Kaisar,* which, using numerical values for the Hebrew letters, also adds up to 666, suggesting Nero as the beast alive again in Domitian. No theory, however, explains why a book written in Greek would switch to Latin, as in the former suggestion, or to Hebrew, in the latter suggestion, especially when one letter of the full Hebrew word must be dropped, or it will total 1005 rather than 666. The latter opinion, held quite widely today, was not thought of in the days of the early church fathers.

Consider another view, one that does not take John to be suggesting a particular man but mankind in general. In the Greek text of Revelation 13:18, there is no article. It is translated in the NIV, "man's number," rather than "*a* man's number" or "the number of *a* man" (KJV). Unregenerate humanity may consider itself perfect, but it never is. Throughout Revelation, seven is the number of perfection, or completeness. Humanism at its best falls short of divine perfection. Six is never seven. God's trinity of perfection is 777. Satan's substitute is 666, or failure after failure after failure. The human number, like the human effort to build a tower of Babel that will reach to Heaven, will fall short again and again and yet again. History's trail is strewn with wreckage of men who were deceived by the great deceiver to believe they did not need God in their plans. Men may set out on white horses to conquer a world (Revelation 6:2), but before their chapter is completed, the "stars in [their] sky" will fall to the ground (6:13).

What does it mean to bear the "mark" (χάραγμα)? The word John uses here is the same word found to refer to the official seal used on commercial documents. In John's day, religious devotees to some pagan god wore the name of the deity they served tatooed on their foreheads. Both slaves and cattle were branded by their owners to make evident that ownership.

The Mark in the Head

It is very possible that John, who drew so much of his imagery from the Old Testament, was thinking of Deuteronomy 6. "These commandments that I give you today are to be upon your hearts.... Tie them as symbols on your hands and bind them on your foreheads" (Deuteronomy 6:6-8). God's Old Testament people, like his New Testament people, were marked in heart, hand, and head. You can tell a Christian from a man of the world, not by some electronic invention, but the fact that he thinks differently. He has "the mind of Christ" (1 Corinthians 2:16). He is marked as belonging to the Savior, for he does not think as men of the world. He goes into the world not "to be served, but to serve" (Mark 10:45). Servanthood as the ideal is the opposite of the world's way of thinking.

While those who belong to the beast have a "mark," χάραγμα, showing ownership, the child of God has a "seal," σφραγίς, indicating not only ownership (2 Corinthians 1:22; John 6:27) but protection (Ephesians 1:13, 14; 4:30; see Ezekiel 9:4). This seal of the Holy Spirit is evident in our thinking.

Revelation shows how important proper thinking is. Its

readers are to "hear it and take to heart what is written in it" (Revelation 1:3). They are to distinguish between the doctrine of Christ and the "teaching of Balaam" (Revelation 2:14) or the "teaching of the Nicolaitans" (Revelation 2:15). Much of the appeal Satan offers, to lure the saved from the simplicity that is in Christ, is to offer "Satan's so-called deep secrets" (Revelation 2:24). Truth and error are not to be equals in the house of God.

No one can read Revelation, or any of the Biblical books that precede it, and say doctrine does not matter. Christ is Lord. What He taught and what His inspired apostles and prophets taught and wrote on any issue must take precedence. As Peter and John said, so long ago, "Judge for yourselves whether it is right in God's sight to obey you rather than God" (Acts 4:19). A disciple's mind agrees with the words of his Teacher as to Christ's deity and as to His terms. They cannot be improved upon. They do not need to be updated by further findings. His gospel is eternal and unchanging. Believers from century one to century twenty-one have the same mind. The mark is indelible.

The Mark in the Hand

Isaiah foretold how "one will say, 'I belong to the Lord'; ... still another will write on his hand, 'the Lord's'" (Isaiah 44:5). Moses, at the ordinance of the Passover, said the observance of the annual feast "will be for you like a sign on your hand and a reminder on your forehead" (Exodus 13:9). He meant that Jewish thoughts and actions were to glorify God. That kind of Old Testament thinking prepared John's readers to understand what he meant by saying each follower of the beast would bear "a mark on his right hand or on his forehead" (Revelation 13:16). To whom you have sold yourself, body, soul, and spirit, will show in deeds and concepts, in practice and profession, in works and words.

The mark of the best is evident in the lives of the blest. They have a life-style that is instantly recognizable as different. Not only "where the Scriptures speak" do they speak, but "where the Scriptures speak" do they act. Look at their hands as they reach out to the poor and the needy (James 1:27). Look at their hands as they extend help to the lost. Look at their hands as they grasp out to hold on to a brother getting too close to a dangerous precipice.

No follower of the beast wrote, "I have been crucified with

Christ and I no longer live, but Christ lives in me. The life I live in the body, I live by faith in the Son of God, who loved me and gave himself for me" (Galatians 2:20). No one deceived by the false prophet called on men to "offer [their] bodies as living sacrifices, holy and pleasing to God" (Romans 12:1). No individuals allured by the great harlot confessed, "Christ's love compels us, because we are convinced that one died for all, and therefore all died. And he died for all, that those who live should no longer live for themselves but for him who died for them and was raised again" (2 Corinthians 5:14, 15).

A form of Christianity more acceptable to the deceiver would be less demanding. It would not draw such clear lines. It would sound more reasonable and be more eclectic. A pale Galilean would be less disturbing in the world than the one described in Revelation. John's Jesus condemns theft, idolatry, falsehood, and uncleanness. John's Lord asks for courage, zeal, patience, and endurance. Steadfastness marks the hands and heads of Christ's followers. That quality seals their future.

It would be easy to visualize that the mark on the hand and the head reveals an inner mark on the heart. He who perseveres in wrong teachings, wrong life-styles, and wrong attitudes is marked for condemnation. The world's deliverance requires moral redemption, as well as political and religious deliverance. It starts within, "for out of the heart come . . . what make a man 'unclean'" (Matthew 15:19, 20).

Revelation encourages all who are on the front line to expect tribulation while extending the kingdom and never to lose "patience." Such steadfastness will be theirs when they rely on their Savior's vows to them and are undeceived by the serpent's voice. Let them remember they are marked to receive the saint's victory.

The Perspective of Universal Worship

CHAPTER FIVE

The Perspective of Universal Worship

"On the Lord's Day . . . in the Spirit . . . a loud voice"

The "rapture" is an intriguing theme. Especially so if you mean the rapture of a "Lord's Day"—a Sunday worship service where God's saints have assembled to praise Him. What an enrapturing experience! What a foretaste of eternity!

Compare the key verses, Revelation 1:9, 10, to a pair of binoculars. The ninth verse is the lens through which we have looked to see the suffering, victory, and steadfastness of Christ's church in its mission for "the word of God and the testimony of Jesus." The tenth verse is the other lens, through which we now view this great book by John. It is the lens of worship. To look through verse 9 is to see prophecy. To focus in with verse 10 is to view praise.

"On the Lord's Day I was in the Spirit," wrote John. Modern writers correctly see this as a liturgical suggestion.

The "Lord's Day" is not "the day of the Lord," the final day, the day of judgment for the wicked and the day of deliverance for the righteous. Yet every first day of the week is preparation for that coming day of the Lord. When believers across the world gather on Sundays and sing their hymns, that is choir practice for that future day when all the redeemed will sing praise to their Redeemer. The gathered church, on the day commemorating Christ's resurrection, could be said to be another wedding rehearsal for the marriage feast in glory (Revelation 19:7). Perhaps the Bible study each week could be considered the preparation of the disciples of Jesus for the eventual final exam. If musicians practice for the coming concert and ball players drill for the big game, Christians could be looked at as those in preparation for eternity.

John received his visions on a Lord's Day, when the Aegean waters separated him from his flock in Asia. He was absent from their assembly by the imperial interference of Rome. What he saw, recorded, and sent to the congregations across Asia would also be read to them on a Lord's Day—the day of Christian assembly.

That the first day of the week is what John had in mind when he penned the words "Lord's Day" is evident by reading how the early church spoke of their day for corporate worship. A glance into the *Didache,* or *The Teaching of the Twelve Apostles,*[18] Ignatius,[19] and others will settle any doubts about that. How else would the word for Sunday have come into the Romance languages in words that mean Lord's Day, such as the Italian *domenico,* the Spanish *domingo* or the French *dimanche.* Where Romans, in the time of John, set aside the first day of the month to recognize the Caesar as "lord," the Christian kept the first day of the week in recognition of the fact that Jesus' resurrection on that day had established that He was Lord indeed.

Προσκευνέω, the verb meaning "to worship" or "to kiss the hand toward another," is found a few times in the Gospels and Acts (thirteen times in Matthew, twice in Mark, nine times in John, and seven times in both Luke and Acts), but twenty-four times in Revelation. This indicates the high priority the book places on worship. (See Revelation 19:10.) The object of one's worship is that in which he or she places the highest worth or considers of the highest value.

Revelation is rich in calls to worship and scenes of praise. Antiphonal choirs sing, and elders encourage adoration of the Lamb. Listen to the hymns of praise to God as Creator in chapter 5. Give ear to the songs to Jesus as Redeemer in chapter 6. Hear what Handel heard in the music of chapter 19 to inspire his "Hallelujah Chorus." Recognize that the resounding praise from one side of Heaven to the other is the consequence of the church's obedience to the Great Commission. That great choir "that no one could count" is comprised of the saved "from every nation, tribe, people and language" (Revelation 7:9).

The harvested souls gathered by the soul winners of the world understand the significance of the "Lord's Day," the importance

---

[18] *Didache* 10:6.

[19] Ignatius *to Magnesium* 9:1.

of the Lord's "Spirit," and the vital place of the Lord's "voice" in the worship experience of the believer. Jesus earlier had told His followers, "A time is coming and has now come when the true worshipers will worship the Father in spirit and truth, for they are the kind of worshipers the Father seeks" (John 4:23). That is to say, worship pleasing to God requires both the proper object and a correct attitude. It is to be done also in the right way. Revelation has the same liturgical counsel.

Aflame for the Lord

Who will be lord of your life? There can be only one. Who alone is worthy of your worship? "No one can serve two masters. Either he will hate the one and love the other, or he will be devoted to the one and despise the other. You cannot serve God and Money" (Matthew 6:24). We all recognize that we can serve God with money, but a good servant must never become our master.

The book of our study was written by a monotheist. Christians will not bow down to an emperor. They will not bow the knee to angels, demons, or the devil. But, unanimously and gladly, they cast their crowns and their lives at the feet of Jesus, for they know who He is. Jesus is Lord.

Review what you know well. The Ten Commandments to Israel began, "I am the Lord your God, who brought you out of Egypt, out of the land of slavery. You shall have no other gods before [besides] me" (Exodus 20:2, 3). This was a call for total allegiance. Jesus, in the wilderness of temptation, struck back at Satan's request for worship with the response, "Away from me, Satan! For it is written: 'Worship the Lord your God, and serve him only'" (Matthew 4:10). When Cornelius, the Roman centurion, fell at Peter's feet, the soldier received the apostle's rebuke. "'Stand up,' he said, 'I am only a man myself'" (Acts 10:26). Paul and Barnabas, upon becoming recipients of garlands and oxen from the Lystrians, cried out, "Men, why are you doing this? We too are only men, human like you. We are bringing you good news, telling you to turn from these worthless things to the living God" (Acts 14:15). They tore their garments, disturbed by men who could not distinguish between the Creator and that which He has created, or the messengers and the one about whom their message speaks.

After the emphasis of the first twenty-one chapters of

Revelation, that only the divine is worthy of worship, John himself made the dreadful error of falling down before the angel that showed him the visions. Promptly and properly, he received the correction: "Do not do it! I am a fellow servant with you and with your brothers the prophets and of all who keep the words of this book. Worship God!" (Revelation 22:9).

From the first book of the Bible to the last, and from the beginning words of Revelation to the final conclusion, we are warned against polytheistic thinking. There is but one supreme power. To Him alone is our total loyalty to be given.

In A.D. 96, Domitian insisted on being called *deus ad dominus,* god and lord.[20] These very words that Thomas called Jesus after the resurrection (John 20:28), an earthly emperor demanded for himself upon penalty of death. John likely refers to this situation the church was facing as he described the world worshiping the beast (Revelation 13:4, 8, 15; 14:9, 11; 16:2; 19:20) and the second beast encouraging that worship (13:12). The earlier Syrian, Antiochus Epiphanes, by his very name, considered himself worthy of worship, for *Epiphanes* means God manifest. Julius Caesar liked being called the "divine Julius." Augustus Caesar considered himself "august," and thus the one to have the final say. To call an emperor "your worship" was an expected gesture of gratitude for the *pax Romana* and good conditions Rome's subjects enjoyed.

Those who sat at the feet of Jesus learned to appreciate good emperors, but they would not deify them. They would gladly pray *for* the Roman Caesar, but they would die before praying *to* him. Other citizens may say, "Caesar is lord." Citizens of God's kingdom only confess "Christ is Lord."

Monotheistic Christians will not worship Caesars or demons (Revelation 9:20) or angels (22:8, 9) or even the finest of men (5:3, 4). Let believers never forget that their beloved pastors and elders may have clay feet. Their perfect message is not to be rejected should any flaw be found in the messengers. The only one found worthy to open the book, after searching Heaven and earth and under the earth, was God's Lamb (Revelation 5:2-5). Only Jesus is worthy or deserving of man's adoration.

John presented, in his pages, the reasons he believed Christ

---

[20] Suetonius: *Domitian* 13; Irenaeus: *Against Heresies* 5.

deserves the world's allegiance. Those traversing the earth with the gospel hold forth the same case for consideration. If a man can have but one supreme Lord, why should the name of Jesus on the long slate of candidates receive his single vote?

John points to Christ's character as rationale for our worship. He is "the Alpha and the Omega . . . who is, and who was, and who is to come, the Almighty" (Revelation 1:8). If Revelation 1:8 calls the Father the Alpha and the Omega, Revelation 22:13 calls the Son by the exact same terms. He is no mortal. He is rather "the First and the Last. . . . the Living One . . . alive for ever and ever" (1:17, 18). He is not a fearsome dictator whose love of power led Him to use people, destroy hopes, and spread evil. He is, rather, that benevolent Savior whose power of love deserves the adoration of "Holy, holy, holy" (4:8) or the praise of "Great and marvelous are your deeds. . . . Just and true are your ways. . . . For you alone are holy. Your righteous acts have been revealed" (15:3, 4).

Symbolically portrayed, the Messiah, garbed as high priest, had white hair and eyes "like blazing fire" (1:14). He had antiquity and omniscience. Feet "like bronze glowing in a furnace" tell of His omnipotence. His voice, "like the sound of rushing waters," reveals the authority of His Word (1:15). The rest of His description, here and throughout, attribute to Him titles and deeds that were the titles and deeds of Jehovah throughout the Old Testament. No wonder the living creatures and elders joined the angels of "thousands upon thousands, and ten thousand times ten thousand," as they sang in a loud voice, "Worthy is the Lamb, who was slain, to receive power and wealth and wisdom and strength and honor and glory and praise" (5:11, 12). The seven-fold ascriptions of worship to Christ in Revelation 5:12 are equal to the seven-fold doxology to the Father in 7:12.

Christ and the Father both are enthroned (Revelation 22:1, 3) and share sovereignty (11:15). Both give grace and peace (1:4, 5) and search the human heart (2:23). Both are first and last (22:13) and titled the Living One (1:18). Both are holy and true (3:7). Paul found no hesitation in bowing "every knee" to the Incarnate One (Philippians 2:9-11), for the "mystery" is that God "appeared in a body" (1 Timothy 3:16). Jesus is made known by twenty-six different titles in Revelation. Each exalts Him to His rightful position.

Christ and Caesar vie for human loyalty. Will it be given to a ravenous beast who takes life or to a gentle Lamb who gives life? One is self-serving and will use you. The other is self-giving and will lift you. The mortal will offer a forced choice. The Eternal One gives you free choice.

Before the choice is made, remember who made you and who bought you back. The hymns of Revelation 4 praise the "Almighty" (4:8) who created all things (4:11). It was by God's "will they were created and have their being" (4:11). The songs of Revelation 5 adore the Lamb who "purchased men for God" with His blood (5:9).

He "who loves us and has freed us from our sins by his blood" (Revelation 1:5) is worthy of our worship. The enemy is overcome "by the blood of the Lamb" (Revelation 12:11) and filthy garments are "washed . . . and made . . . white in the blood of the Lamb" (Revelation 7:14). Is not this Lamb, so titled twenty-nine times in this book, the one whom we should value above all else? Man and human government were symbolized through prophets, from Daniel to John, as some ravenous beast. Jesus and His reign are pictured as Lamb and Shepherd. Shall we crown fearful savagery or sacrificial kindness?

Recognizing Jesus as the instrument of creation (John 1:1-3: Hebrews 1:1, 2; Colossians 1:16) and of redemption, followers of Christ join the four living creatures in saying, "Amen," and the elders who "fell down and worshiped" (5:14).

Jesus is not Michael or some other created angel. He is the Son of God. No better evidence for that fact exists than the Lamb's resurrection from the grave. As John wrote, that historic event has become the Church's proclamation. The Lamb, once slain, is now "standing" (Revelation 5:6) and is become "the Lion of the tribe of Judah" (5:5). He is "the firstborn from the dead" (1:5). He was dead, but now He is "alive for ever and ever." He holds "the keys of death and Hades" (1:18). The confirmation of the Messiah's deity is His resurrection. Paul wrote that Jesus had been "declared with power to be the Son of God by his resurrection from the dead" (Romans 1:4). He referred to the confession made by every convert, that "Jesus is Lord," a confession based on a heartfelt belief that God raised Him from the dead (Romans 10:9). That was the gospel they "preached" and the people "received" (1 Corinthians 15:1-4). That was the good news behind Revelation's picture of Christ as Lord of history.

Is life stronger than death? Is love more powerful than hate? Will truth outlive falsehood? Shall men place their hopes in a charismatic figure who offers some future utopia on earth, or should they make God's Son their Lord for time and eternity? The Christians decided for Christ as Lord (Acts 2:36; Psalm 110:1). They knew His resurrection was followed by His exaltation to the right hand of the Father (Acts 5:31; Romans 8:34; Ephesians 1:20; Colossians 3:1; Hebrews 1:3, 13; 10:12; 12:2; 1 Peter 3:22). Revelation 3:21 contains Christ's promise to overcomers on the basis that He also overcame, and sat down with God on His throne.

The book of the future, held in the hand of God, was completely sealed until Jesus stepped forward as the one "worthy" to open it (Revelation 5:1-10). One by one the "seven seals" are broken, starting at chapter 6, where the future is made known by the crucified, risen, and now reigning Lord. This Lord of love—this Lord of creation and redemption—who has proven to be Lord of death itself, is also Lord of the future time (chapters 6-20) and all eternity (chapters 21, 22).

Let the universe rejoice, saying, "Hallalujah! For our Lord God Almighty reigns" (Revelation 19:6). Let all mankind say, "We give thanks to you, Lord God Almighty ... because you have taken your great power and have begun to reign" (Revelation 11:17). The future belongs to no emperor or ecclesiastic, but to Christ.

The Jesus of the church has been no religious genius or farsighted visionary. He has been no unusual man or rare personality. He has been God enfleshed and involved with men for their rescue from sin. They pray to Him (Revelation 6:10) as well as to the Father, in His name (Ephesians 5:20; Hebrews 13:15). They sing with Isaac Watts, "Joy to the World! the Lord is come." They echo, "All hail the Power of Jesus' name! Let angels prostrate fall: Bring forth the royal diadem, And crown Him Lord of all!"[21] His "name" is referred to forty times in Revelation, for at His name, every knee shall bow.

Every "Lord's Day" for two thousand years, Christians from East and West, North and South have gathered on the resurrection day to worship Him "who is worthy." The Sabbath of Old

---

[21] "All Hail the Power of Jesus' Name" by Edward Peronnet.

Covenant days recalled the wondrous truth of man's creation. The Lord's Day of New Covenant times points to the even more glorious fact that the Creator has become the Redeemer. On such a Lord's Day, John is given the visions of the Apocalypse. No mention is made as to what year it is. It tells not what month it is. Month and year are insignificant to John's purpose. What day it is, however, really matters. It is crammed with significance. It is the first day of the week, Sunday, or the Lord's Day. The last chapters of Matthew, Mark, Luke, and John not only tell the resurrection fact but name "the first day of the week" (Matthew 28:1; Mark 16:2; Luke 24:1; John 20:1). This is so their communities will understand the cause for that day's significance in the church. The greatest fact of all history was Christ's resurrection. The Lord's Day bears witness to that event.

Aglow With the Spirit

For a Sunday worship service to be an enrapturing experience, the worshipers must be aflame for the Lord on whose day they gather. A second ingredient is that each person be aglow with His Spirit. John spoke of being "in the Spirit" on the Lord's Day.

What is the meaning of the phrase "in the Spirit"? Is it not to be under His influence or under His control? Is it not being guided or led by the Spirit? Thus, John asserts that he is under the influence of God's Spirit. According to Paul, those under the influence of intoxicating wines sing ribald songs at some orgy, but those "filled with the Spirit speak to one another with psalms, hymns and spiritual songs" (Ephesians 5:18, 19). He also requested that believers "pray in the Spirit [or as God's Spirit guides] on all occasions" (Ephesians 6:18).

"In the Spirit," Epaphras declared the Colossians' love for Paul and Timothy (Colossians 1:8), and "by the Spirit" the Philippians worshiped (Philippians 3:3). The same Holy Spirit who had given apocalyptic visions to Ezekiel of old (Ezekiel 3:12, 14; 8:3; 11:24; 37:1; 43:5) lifted John's spirit on the Patmos Isle. That same Spirit indwells all Christians everywhere (Romans 8:9). And while He may not reveal apocalyptic visions today, He does make times of worship, even in the humblest of settings, enrapturing experiences.

Silence

Where the Spirit guides our worship, there will be "silence"

(Revelation 8:1). Habakkuk (2:20) admonished: "Let all the earth be silent before him." The Psalmist had Jehovah encouraging His people with the words: "Be still, and know that I am God" (Psalm 46:10). Isaiah's plea for silence before God is well known: "This is what the Sovereign Lord, the Holy One of Israel, says: '... In quietness and trust is your strength'" (Isaiah 30:15).

Centuries of experience have proven the value of quietness before the Lord in preparation for receiving His message. As the hymn writer prayed, so do our hearts:

> "Drop Thy still dews of quietness,
> Till all our strivings cease;
> Take from our souls the strain and stress,
> And let our ordered lives confess
> The beauty of Thy peace." [22]

Receptivity

There is something about silence that is conducive to worship. Busy people need to be quiet so the Spirit can prepare them to be receptive of God's grace. Have you noticed that the last sentence John wrote has the word "grace" in it? "The grace of the Lord Jesus be with God's people" (Revelation 22:21). He began the book with the same word. "John, To the seven churches in the province of Asia: Grace and peace to you" (Revelation 1:4).

A worship service is not an assembly in which people have gathered to report all the great things they have done. Far from it. The flock of God gathers to express gratitude for being recipients of the Lord's marvelous grace. Their blessing comes from the fact that they "hunger and thirst for righteousness," and hence are "filled" (Matthew 5:6). The beatitudes of the Sermon on the Mount show the blessedness that a Savior can be to a recipient who knows his own spiritual poverty but his Master's abundant grace (Matthew 5:3-12). The seven beatitudes in the book of Revelation (1:3; 14:13; 16:15; 19:9; 20:6; 22:7, 14) point to God's unmerited favor richly bestowed upon all who will reach out to receive.

Listening

Once the hurricane of a bustling week subsides into quietness

---

[22] "Dear Lord and Father of Mankind" by John G. Whittier.

and the heart is readied to receive, God speaks to the listening ears. "Blessed is the one who reads the words of this prophecy, and blessed are those who hear it and take to heart what is written in it." So reads the first beatitude of the book (Revelation 1:3). The call to listen is repeated over and over. "He who has an ear, let him hear what the Spirit says to the churches" (Revelation 2:7, 11, 17, 29; 3:6, 13, 22).

Taking in God's Word is compared to eating a meal (Revelation 10:8-10). No meal, physical or spiritual, can be so abundant that the next meal will not be needed for another six months or a year. The New Testament church knew that and, therefore, "they devoted themselves to the apostles' teaching" (Acts 2:42). Behind the human voice of the teacher was heard the voice of the Good Shepherd (John 10:27). "The revelation of Jesus Christ, which God gave him to show his servants" (Revelation 1:1) can be called the word of the church, the Word of God, the Word of Christ, or the Word of the Spirit (Revelation 2:7). Call it what you will. In every land, the persons who have responded to the call of Christ gather on the Lord's Day to hear afresh His voice.

Introspection and Prayer

After John had been told to consume the book, he was next given "a reed like a measuring rod" and was instructed to "go and measure the temple of God and the altar, and count the worshipers there" (Revelation 11:1). As John wrote, he knew the Jewish temple had been destroyed some twenty-six years earlier. He recognized that the physical building in Jerusalem had been but a type of the church, for in the gospel age, God dwells in His people. Whatever else the passage implies, from the vantage point of worship, it suggests that, upon taking in God's message, it is time for introspection. Are we measuring up? No worshiper will be lifted up by the service on a Lord's Day who does not seek to measure up to the plumb line of truth.

Self-examination leads in a straight line to prayer. John refers to prayer by using the imagery of "golden bowls full of incense," which he says "are the prayers of the saints" (Revelation 5:8). As the aroma of the "incense" penetrated the veil separating the Old Testament temple's "holy place" from the cubical "holy of holies," a believer's prayers reach beyond what human eyes can see into Heaven itself. The bowls are golden to indicate how precious such intercessions are to God.

Under fire, some of John's friends may have thought their requests were bouncing off the ceiling and getting no higher. He points out to them that the trumpet angels, who will go forth according to chapters 8-11, will go in response to the church's intercession to God. Unto the angel, John writes, "was given much incense to offer, with the prayers of all the saints, on the golden altar before the throne. The smoke of the incense, together with the prayers of the saints, went up before God from the angel's hand" (Revelation 8:3, 4).

No one can fail to see that God's priests on earth may be despised and rejected of men, yet in God's eyes their prayers are as precious as gold and as sweet as incense. The judgments that come upon the earth are attributed to the accumulative power of prayer. Sufferers in Rome, like the Israelites in Egypt, receive reprieve, for their cries are heard. They had been pleading, "How long, Sovereign Lord, holy and true, until you judge the inhabitants of the earth and avenge our blood?" (Revelation 6:10). Let not the people of God attribute the course of history to blind chance. Prayer changes things. The gathered church on the Lord's Day is in a prayer meeting. Their intercession is not inconsequential. The Lord of history hears. The Lord of the church acts. The fruitful results, across the mission fields of the world, are the consequence of the united prayers of kingdom people.

Praise and Giving

Joined together in John's vision were golden bowls and musical harps. The former pictured prayer and the latter praise. He who sees the answer to his prayers cannot but rejoice and be thankful. "Each one had a harp" (Revelation 5:8). "They sang a new song" (5:9). They made a sound "like that of harpists playing their harps" (Revelation 14:2). The grateful sound is not from the unredeemed, for praise is from the saved who have the "harps given them by God" (Revelation 15:2). Jesus had described the fitting sound coming from the house of God to be that of "music and dancing" (Luke 15:25), for prodigals, received back by their Heavenly Father, have to "celebrate and be glad" because they are "alive again" and "found" (Luke 15:32). No single harp accompanied the many singers. Every singer had reason to be grateful. All had been saved by grace. All sang their praise.

The adoration and praise to God in Revelation is not out of duty but out of a loving gratitude that refuses to be suppressed. Spontaneously, creatures fall at His feet (Revelation 1:17) or shout, "Amen, Hallelujah!" (Revelation 19:4).

Christians have much to celebrate, and music has become their chief channel of praise. The psalms, hymns, and spiritual songs (Ephesians 5:19; Colossians 3:16), named by Paul, show themselves in his epistles (1 Timothy 3:16; Philippians 2:5-10; Ephesians 5:14). Similar early church music is heard in the chapters of John's writing (Revelation 4:8, 11; 5:9, 10, 12, 13; 11:15, 16-18; 12:10-12, 14:7; 15:3, 4; 19:1, 2, 5, 6-8). Besides hymns, there are calls to worship, postures of worship, instruments related to worship, and acts of giving—the highest form of praise.

Hear John's description of worship at its highest: "Whenever the living creatures give glory, honor and thanks to him who sits on the throne and who lives for ever and ever, the twenty-four elders fall down before him who sits on the throne, and worship him who lives for ever and ever. They lay their crowns before the throne" (Revelation 4:9, 10). Such an act of giving recognizes that salvation is a result of God's unmerited favor. We contributed nothing that deserved His blessings. But we give of our time and lives in His service because of gratitude for His gift unspeakable.

In the Bible's first book, we look for man's first act of worship. It was not a baptismal service. It was not a communion service with bread and wine. It was not an organ concert, choir cantata, or congregational songfest with closing devotions. The first act of worship recorded was the bringing of an offering (Genesis 4:3-5). Many facts of the Genesis story come to mind in the reading of Revelation. As in the first book, so in the last, the bringing of an offering to lay before the Lord is worship indeed.

Alert to the Voice

To be in the Spirit on the Lord's Day (Revelation 1:10), the worshiper must be a participant. In every successful baseball game, there are both pitchers and catchers. Football requires quarterbacks with good arms and receivers with good hands. The church service leaves much to be desired that has a preacher ready to proclaim God's message but a congregation not in a receptive frame of mind. You will be blessed, indeed, each weekly assembly, if you can say on that first day of the week:

"This is 'the Lord's Day,' and I am 'in the Spirit,' having the right attitude. Now I am ready to listen to the voice of Christ speak to me."

John wrote, "On the Lord's Day ... I heard behind me a loud voice like a trumpet" (Revelation 1:10). He adds, "I turned around to see the voice that was speaking to me" (1:12). There follows the symbolic description of Jesus garbed as the church's high priest (1:13-16).

The saying, *Vox populi, vox dei,* or, "The voice of the people is the voice of the gods," will not suffice for the Christians. God's people listen not for the opinions of men nor the words of the dragon (Revelation 13:11), but for the voice of their shepherd. Once the question is answered, "Is Jesus Lord?" the following inquiry is: "Has Christ spoken?" *Lord* implies *slave.* "Don't you know that when you offer yourselves to someone to obey him as slaves, you are slaves to the one whom you obey" (Romans 6:16), wrote Paul. "Why do you call me, 'Lord, Lord,' and do not do what I say?" (Luke 6:46), asked Jesus.

To call Christ "Lord" is to stand at attention waiting for orders. The human will is bowing before the divine will, praying, "Your will be done." What does the Master desire?

You are not likely to give your mother a box of cigars for Mother's Day. Wanting to please her, you find that gift she would appreciate. You will give to the object of your love what she enjoys. This instructs me not to seek the kind of worship service that I will enjoy. Christ is the object of my adoration. What does He seek from me in the hour of worship? Revelation 11:1 suggests that His voice calls for me to do some measuring. "I was given a reed like a measuring rod and was told, 'Go and measure the temple of God.'"

The first-century church understood that the tabernacle of old, and its later counterpart, the temple in Jerusalem, was God's type for the church. The type was temporary, but the antitype is eternal. Exactness was important in constructing the "tent of meeting" because of the lasting truths it foreshadowed. The author of Hebrews called the tabernacle "a copy and shadow of what is in heaven." He then reminded his readers how important was the exact following of the instructions. He said, "Moses was warned when he was about to build the tabernacle: 'See to it that you make everything according to the pattern shown you on the mountain'" (Hebrews 8:5).

If God desired careful construction according to blueprint for the type, He certainly cares about the antitype. "Don't you know that you yourselves are God's temple and that God's Spirit lives in you? ... God's temple is sacred, and you are that temple" (1 Corinthians 3:16, 17). "In him the whole building is joined together and rises to become a holy temple in the Lord. And in him you too are being built together to become a dwelling in which God lives by his Spirit" (Ephesians 2:19-22). With such a high theology of the church, John wrote Revelation. Neither God nor His church is small. The church is universal. Each local congregation is worshiping with God's creatures in Heaven as well as His elect on earth. There is something very personal about the praise, but nothing is private. The saints from Ephesus and Smyrna were one in their adoration of Christ with martyrs and angels. Sectarian thought or private individualism is swallowed up in the universal worship Revelation heralds.

The "temple" in Revelation 11 that Christ's voice asks us to measure had within it a table, an altar of incense, and a candelabrum, even as the church has the Lord's table of Communion, the prayers of its saints, and the light of its gospel.

Measuring Table, Altar, and Lampstand

The "table of the presence" was reset every week. It had on it unleavened bread and cups of wine. Many consider that table in the tabernacle to be a picture of the Lord's Supper in the church. Some liturgists think that this weekly feast in the first century church was in John's mind as he wrote to the gathered congregations across Asia. His words, "Come, Lord Jesus" (Revelation 22:20), that close his letter are compared to *"Maranatha,"* or "Come, O Lord!" that conclude Paul's first Corinthian letter (1 Corinthians 16:22). Both may be prayers for Jesus to be present at the Lord's Supper, which immediately would have followed the reading of apostolic correspondence.

We also are asked to consider the promise of Revelation 3:20 as a Communion promise. It is the congregation of believers who are told, "Here I am! I stand at the door and knock. If anyone hears my voice and opens the door, I will come in and eat with him, and he with me." The Supper of the Lord on the Lord's Day is considered but a foretaste of the Heavenly banquet, "the wedding supper of the Lamb" (Revelation 19:9).

The Jesus of Revelation is the one who died on the cross, is reigning now, and is coming in the future. These facts we remember at the Table of the Lord. While supping with Him, we are to discern the body (1 Corinthians 11:29) as Revelation 2 and 3 bids us to do.

Does your presence and self-examination at the Table measure up to the desire of Him who has bidden you to come? At the altar of incense, have your prayers been acceptable to Him? That altar was just before the curtain dividing the two parts of the tabernacle. This has led to the observation that in prayer, one is as close to Heaven as possible while still on earth. Do you recognize the candelabrum as the only light for those in the temple? This picture prophecy suggests that worshipers in God's church walk in the light of God's revelation. Seven vials of oil, with seven flaming wicks, speak of the completeness of that Holy Spirit-inspired truth. No skylights or windows are needed to let in other truths by which to walk. The number seven speaks to the total adequacy of the revelation God has provided. John hears the Heavenly voice call for measuring. Does the teaching on the Lord's Day measure up to what the Lord of the Lord's Day has given? Has anything been added, taken away, or altered? This is no unimportant question. It was asked early in the Biblical material (Deuteronomy 4:2; 12:32), at the center (Proverbs 30:6), and now again at the end (Revelation 22:18, 19).

When the gospel goes to people with different languages and with totally different backgrounds, what will keep it from becoming so modified by the culture that it is in no way like the faith in other places? The Word of Christ to all His sheep is that they hear His voice and follow Him (John 10:27). In the figure of Revelation 11, Christ's object is to continue to measure all life and teaching by the yardstick He has provided. That measuring is to include the altar.

Measuring Sacrifice, Laver, and Ministry

On going into the tabernacle, the priest would first pass the altar of sacrifice, bathe in the laver, and then enter the holy place. We are the priests (Revelation 1:6). Our becoming such began when we were confronted by the Christ of the cross, the Lamb of God offered for the sacrifice of the world. Hearing that story of blood atonement, and accepting the gospel that an innocent and spotless vicarious Lamb died in our place, we next went to the laver. Paul called baptism the laver, that is, the "washing" of regeneration (Ephesians 5:26; Titus 3:5; note Hebrews 10:22). The symbolism is that, believing in the cleansing blood of Christ and washing in the laver, we enter the church, or holy place, where we serve our Lord forever. In the eternal tomorrows, beyond the veil, "His servants will serve him" (Revelation 22:3). John spoke of Christ's slaves carrying on religious duties, eternally. Such service does not begin after we go beyond the veil separating earth and Heaven. It commences upon our ordination to ministry at the waters of baptism. Jesus' ministry began at His baptism. Those who follow Him enter the priesthood of believers and begin to serve their Lord at their baptism.

The task left to the Lord's church on earth is evangelism and the nurturing of the evangelized so they can join in the mission. "The Spirit and the bride say, 'Come!'" That is, Christ is present in His church, and they extend Heaven's call to the lost. But it does not stop there. The concluding call is, "And let him who hears say 'Come!'" In other words, each convert is to make converts. The church is to multiply. John goes on, "Whoever is thirsty, let him come." No roadblock is to be placed in the way of any person for whom Christ died. No racial barriers or class barriers are to make it difficult for any prodigal to come home. "Whoever wishes, let him take the free gift of the water of life" (Revelation 22:17).

With such a conclusion, Revelation demands evangelism. Let the church pray for spiritual health and divide not its energies. The call of Jesus was for those who believed in His resurrection to "Go into all the world and preach the good news to all creation" (Mark 16:15). That same call echoes across the twenty-two chapters of Revelation. Let every disciple of Christ on each Lord's Day become newly aflame for his Lord, aglow with His Spirit, and alert to His voice as it cries, "Go!" How else will there ever be enough voices to sing His praise?

CONCLUSION
MISSION ACCOMPLISHED

Neither the word *mission,* nor *missionary* is found in an English translation of Revelation, or for that matter, in any other New Testament book. Yet the overriding concern throughout Revelation is getting out the "word of God and the testimony of Jesus" (Revelation 1:9) so that all men hear "the Spirit and the bride say, 'Come!'" (22:17).

Doors of opportunity to evangelize can be opened that none can shut (Revelation 3:7). It is vital that, before "Satan will be released from his prison" for "a short time" (20:3, 7), every church recover its "first love" and penitently return to its "first works" of sharing its faith. The most distinctive difference between Christianity and the other world religions is its concept of God searching for man. It is more than God's willingness to accept back men who had broken willingly from Him. It is the insatiable hunger of God's heart to seek and to find each one of His creatures. No sin is big enough to bar a human from Heaven. Christ's shed blood will cover every evil thought and deed. Stubborn defiance of God's gracious offer is the only thing that can keep God's creatures from entering the holy city.

Revelation, like the rest of sacred Scripture, knows nothing of "ten lost tribes." But it knows how lost is every Jew and Gentile of each tribe, tongue, and people. Doom is announced for all who follow the beast. Hope is heralded for all who will follow Christ. "Blessed" are the readers who "take to heart what is written . . . because the time is near" (Revelation 1:3). How long do we have before the day of salvation turns into the day of judgment? The question "How long?" receives the answer, "Until the number of their fellow servants and brothers who were to be killed as they had been was completed" (Revelation 6:10, 11). The implication is that, as Christ suffered to make man's salvation possible, Christians in their mission of getting that story out will face pain until the day of grace concludes. The fellowship of Christ's suffering shared by all in His mission is the cost of God's love.

Because "God so loved the world" (John 3:16), the preaching of the "testimony of Jesus Christ" (Revelation 1:9) must continue. Because "God so loved the world," His people become partakers in whatever tribulation or opposition bearing that message brings. Because "God so loved the world," men are invited to be "brothers in the kingdom." Because "God so loved the world" and wanted no one to "perish" but everyone to find "everlasting life," the church entrusted with that gospel must keep "patience" and remain at the task through every discouragement. "God did not send his Son into the world to condemn the world, but to save the world through him" (John 3:17). When that wish for fallen men finds its fulfillment, the "new song" (Revelation 5:9) will ring forth:

"Great and marvelous are your deeds, Lord God Almighty. Just and true are your ways, King of the ages. Who will not fear you, O Lord, and bring glory to your name? For you alone are holy. All nations will come and worship before you" (Revelation 15:3, 4).

The gospel age began after Christ's Great Commission ordered the discipling of the nations. John's Revelation pulls back the curtain to show how it all will end. In brief, the words are, "Mission Accomplished!"